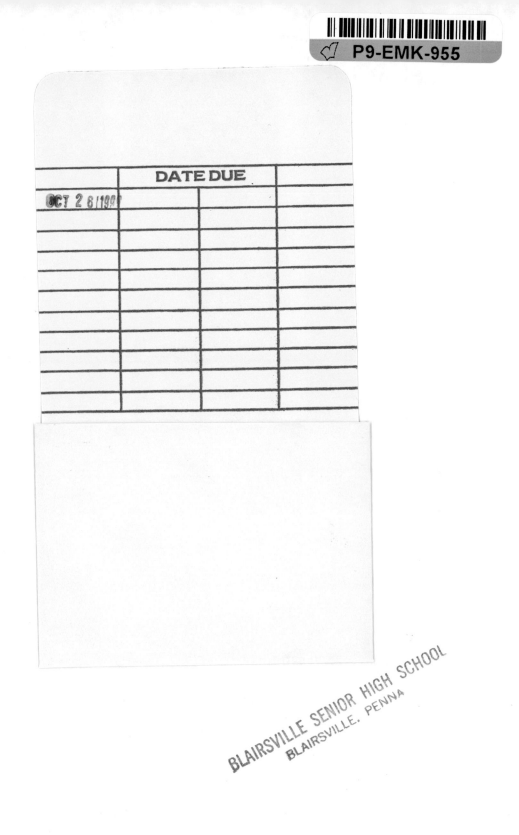

BILL CLINTON

OVERCOMING ADVERSITY

BILL CLINTON

Michael Kelly

Chelsea House Publishers
Philadelphia

Frontis: Listening, learning from others, and keeping an open mind have pulled Bill Clinton through many rough spots in his life. Clinton is shown here on the campaign trail in 1992, connecting with one of his younger supporters.

CHELSEA HOUSE PUBLISHERS

EDITOR IN CHIEF Stephen Reginald
MANAGING EDITOR James D. Gallagher
PRODUCTION MANAGER Pamela Loos
ART DIRECTOR Sara Davis
PICTURE EDITOR Judy L. Hasday
SENIOR PRODUCTION EDITOR Lisa Chippendale

Staff for **Bill Clinton**
SENIOR EDITOR James D. Gallagher
EDITORAL ASSISTANT Laura Gavioli
ASSOCIATE ART DIRECTOR Takeshi Takahashi
DESIGNER Keith Trego
PICTURE RESEARCHER Sandy Jones
COVER ILLUSTRATION Rip Kastaris

First Printing

1 3 5 7 9 8 6 4 2

Library of Congress Cataloging-in-Publication Data

Kelly, Michael.
Bill Clinton / by Michael Kelly.

p. cm. — (Overcoming Adversity)
Includes bibliographical references and index.
Summary: Presents a biography of the forty-second president, who survived a difficult childhood with an abusive stepfather to become the youngest governor of Arkansas and serve two terms as American president.

ISBN 0-7910-4700-8 — ISBN 0-7910-4701-6 (pbk.)
1. Clinton, Bill, 1946- —Juvenile literature. 2. Presidents—United States—Biography—Juvenile literature. [1. Clinton, Bill, 1946- . 2. Presidents.] I. Title. II. Series.
E886.K45 1998
973.929'092—dc21   98-13775
[b]   CIP
                                                               AC

CONTENTS

OVERCOMING ADVERSITY

TIM ALLEN
comedian/performer

JIM CARREY
comedian/performer

BILL CLINTON
U.S. President

JAMES EARL JONES
actor

ABRAHAM LINCOLN
U.S. President

WILLIAM PENN
Pennsylvania's founder

ROSEANNE
entertainer

ON FACING ADVERSITY

James Scott Brady

I GUESS IT'S a long way from a Centralia, Illinois, train yard to the George Washington University Hospital Trauma Unit. My dad was a yardmaster for the old Chicago, Burlington & Quincy Railroad. As a child, I used to get to sit in the engineer's lap and imagine what it was like to drive that train. I guess I always have liked being in the "driver's seat."

Years later, however, my interest turned from driving trains to driving campaigns. In 1979, former Texas governor John Connally hired me as a press secretary in his campaign for the American presidency. We lost the Republican primary to a former Hollywood star named Ronald Reagan. But I managed to jump over to the Reagan campaign. When Reagan was elected in 1980, I was "sitting in the catbird seat," as humorist James Thurber would say—poised to be named presidential press secretary. I held that title throughout the eight years of the Reagan administration. But not without one terrible, extended interruption.

It happened barely two months after the Reagan administration took office. I never even heard the shots. On March 30, 1981, my life went blank in an instant. In an attempt to assassinate President Reagan, John Hinckley Jr. armed himself with a "Saturday night special"—a low-quality, $29 pistol—and shot wildly as our presidential entourage exited a Washington hotel. One of the exploding bullets struck me just above the left eye. It shattered into a couple dozen fragments, some of which penetrated my skull and entered my brain.

The next few months of my life were a nightmare of repeated surgery, broken contact with the outside world, and a variety of medical complications. More than once, I was very close to death.

The next few years were filled with frustrating struggles to function with a paralyzed right side, struggles to speak and communicate.

To people who face and defeat daunting obstacles, "ambition" is not becoming wealthy or famous or winning elections or awards. Words like "ambition" and "achievement" and "success" take on very different meanings. The objective is just to live, to wake up every morning. The goals are not lofty; they are very ordinary.

My own heroes are ordinary folks—but they accomplish extraordinary things because they try. My greatest hero is my wife, Sarah. She's accomplished a lot of things in life, but two stand out. The first has been the way she has cared for me and our son since I was shot. A tremendous tragedy and burden was dropped unexpectedly into her life, totally beyond her control and without justification. She could have given up; instead, she focused her energies on preserving our family and returning our lives to normal as much as possible. Week by week, month by month, year by year, she has not reached for the miraculous, just for the normal. Yet in focusing on the normal, she has helped accomplish the miraculous.

Her other most remarkable accomplishment, to me, has been spearheading the effort to keep guns out of the hands of criminals and children in America. Opponents call her a "gun grabber"; I call her a national hero. And I am not alone.

After a seven-year battle, during which Sarah and I worked tirelessly to educate the public about the need for stronger gun laws, the Brady Bill became law in 1993. It was a victory, achieved in the face of tremendous opposition, that now benefits all Americans. From the time the law took effect through fall 1997, background checks had stopped 173,000 criminals and other high-risk purchasers from buying handguns, and the law has helped to reduce illegal gun trafficking.

Sarah was not pursuing fame, or even recognition. She simply started at one point—when our son, Scott, found a loaded handgun on the seat of a pickup truck and, thinking it was a toy, pointed it at Sarah.

Fortunately, no one was hurt. But seeing a gun nearly bring a second tragedy upon our family, Sarah became determined to do whatever she could to prevent senseless death and injury from guns.

Some people think of Sarah as a powerful political force. To me, she's the person who so many times fed me and helped me dress during my long years of recovery.

Overcoming obstacles is part of life, not just for people who are challenged by disabilities, illnesses, or tragedies, but for all people. No matter what the obstacle—fear, disability, prejudice, grief, or a difficulty that isn't likely to "just go away"—we can all work to make this world a better place.

William J. Clinton is sworn in as the 42nd president of the United States. During his inaugural address, he made a commitment to service for all Americans.

1

THE BABY BOOMER PRESIDENT

AT 11:59 A.M. on January 20, 1993, William Jefferson Clinton took the oath of office of the president of the United States, becoming the nation's 42nd chief executive. At age 46, Bill Clinton was only a few years older than one of his heroes, John F. Kennedy, had been when he succeeded Dwight D. Eisenhower as president in 1961. Clinton, as Kennedy had before him, represented a political coming of age for a new generation: the "baby boomers" born in the years following World War II.

The presidential race of 1992 represented a passage of the reins of government from one generation to the next. At Kennedy's inauguration in 1961 the young president told the nation, "The torch has been passed to a new generation of Americans—born in this century, tempered by war, disciplined by a hard bitter peace, proud of our ancient heritage. . . ."

President Bush, whom Clinton defeated in the 1992 election, was a member of Kennedy's generation, which had come of age during the Great Depression and World War II. The people of this generation found in the presidency of Franklin D. Roosevelt proof that "big government" worked. Roosevelt's New Deal programs had reshaped the nation and stood as a tribute to the positive aspects of federal involvement in American life for over half a century.

Bill Clinton's generation had come of age during the Vietnam conflict, which divided the country and drove a wedge between the various sectors of American society. The presidential administration of Richard Nixon, which coincided with the war and ended in the Watergate scandal, added to the mistrust of government by the baby boomers.

On that chilly morning in January 1993, Bill Clinton's wife, Hillary Rodham Clinton, held a Bible—given to Clinton by his mother—as he took the oath of office, swearing to preserve, protect, and defend the Constitution. Afterward, Clinton made a brief speech to the hundreds attending the ceremony and the millions watching on television. In his 14-minute address, Clinton challenged "a new generation of young Americans to a season of service," saying:

> Today, a generation raised in the shadows of the Cold War assumes new responsibilities in a world warmed by the sunshine of freedom but threatened still by ancient hatreds and new plagues. Raised in unrivaled prosperity, we inherit an economy that is still the world's strongest but is weakened by business failures, stagnant wages, increasing inequality, and deep divisions among our own people. . . .
>
> Though our challenges are fearsome, so are our strengths. . . . From our Revolution to the Civil War, to the Great Depression, to the Civil Rights movement, our people have always mustered the determination to construct from these crises the pillars of our history. Thomas Jefferson believed that to preserve the very foundations of our nation we would need dramatic change from time to time. Well, my fellow Americans, this is our time. Let us embrace it.

His speech also reiterated several of the themes of his campaign, particularly fiscal responsibility. He spoke of the need to "sacrifice" in order to reduce the spiraling federal budget deficit.

A few days earlier, Bill and Hillary Clinton and their 12-year-old daughter Chelsea had arrived in Washington riding the campaign bus that had taken them throughout the entire country during the 1992 presidential campaign; they were accompanied by Vice President-elect Albert Gore and his wife Tipper. The bus's license plate read "Hope1," in recognition both of Bill Clinton's hometown of Hope, Arkansas, and of the new president's approach to life and politics.

On the road to the highest office in American electoral politics, Bill Clinton faced and overcame many challenges in his life, including the death of his father before he was born; his birth into a family of modest means living in one of the poorest states in the nation; and his difficulty with an abusive, alcoholic stepfather when he was growing up. As a young man just out of college and law school, he was an underdog winner in the statewide race for Arkansas's attorney general, and he became the youngest governor in the country when when he was elected in 1978 at age 32. Clinton's career has also included a series of surprising political comebacks, most notably his 1982 reelection victory after a bitter defeat in the 1980 Arkansas gubernatorial race. Even during his lowest points, he never lost hope that he would make the future better.

After the inauguration, Clinton attended several inaugural parties, meeting people and talking about politics. The next morning, filled with ideas for the future, the new president of the United States began the task of reshaping the nation to meet the 21st century.

Together, Bill and Hillary Rodham Clinton have forged a strong political and personal partnership.

A childhood photo of Bill Clinton (right) with his mother, Virginia, and younger brother, Roger Jr. After the death of one father and alcoholic abuse by another, the three struggled to maintain a strong sense of family unity.

2

A TOWN
CALLED HOPE

BILL CLINTON WAS BORN William Jefferson Blythe III on August 19, 1946, in the small farming community of Hope, Arkansas, the only child of William and Virginia Blythe. Billy, as he was called when he was young, would never get to know his father, who died three months before he was born.

His father, William Jefferson Blythe II, was born in the small farming community of Sherman, Texas, in 1918. The sixth child in a family of nine, he was named after his own father. His parents raised their children, along with cotton, corn, and chickens, on their 40-acre farm. However, money was tight for farmers in the 1930s, at the height of the Great Depression, and when Bill Blythe was 13, he started working an eight-hour shift at a local dairy after school to earn extra money for the family.

Like hundreds of thousands of farmers throughout the country during the Great Depression, the Blythe family was helped by an emergency loan from the Agricultural Adjustment Administration, one of the many New Deal agencies established by President Franklin D. Roosevelt to help the nation's farmers.

15

However, when Bill Blythe's father died of colon cancer in 1933, the 15-year-old was forced to quit school in the eighth grade and work as a mechanic to support the family. Unfortunately, the Blythes' federal loan was not enough to pay all the bills, and soon after Bill's father died, the bank foreclosed the mortgage and forced the family off the land.

Bill's mother moved into town and found a position as a hotel maid, and Bill, like many other farm boys during the Great Depression, took to the road. A likable, talkative glad-hander, Bill was always ready with a smile, story, or compliment, and he easily found work as a traveling salesman. His sales route took him throughout Texas, Louisiana, and Arkansas and as far west as California during the late 1930s.

Following the Japanese attack on Pearl Harbor on December 7, 1941, and the United States's subsequent declaration of war, Bill, like millions of other young men, was inducted into the U.S. Army. He was in Shreveport, Louisiana, awaiting orders to ship overseas when he met Virginia Cassidy.

In 1943 Virginia Dell Cassidy was a 20-year-old nursing student finishing her second year of study. She had grown up in Bodcaw, Arkansas, a hamlet of about 100 people that was located in the southwestern part of the state. Virginia was the only daughter of Edith Valeria Grisham and Eldridge Cassidy, working-class Arkansans. The Cassidys, along with millions of other Americans, had been hard hit by the stock market crash of 1929 and the Great Depression that followed. The family lost their home to the bank and was forced to rent a much smaller place on the outskirts of town. Eldridge Cassidy worked at any job that was available and for many years was the town's iceman. In time he saved enough money to open his own general store in Hope, Arkansas. Years later Virginia wrote about the hardship the family faced in the decade prior to World War II and recalled her father breaking down in tears because he could not afford to buy her a new Easter dress.

Virginia's mother Edith was the driving force in the Cassidy household. Where Eldridge Cassidy was talkative, kind, gentle, and good-humored, Edith was stern and unforgiving with family and friends alike. Not content with her lot in life, Edith enrolled in a correspondence school and soon earned a degree as a practical nurse. Her drive and ambition would one day become a strong influence on her grandson, and Bill Clinton would later credit Edith Cassidy with instilling in him a desire to better himself through education. But Edith also had a bad temper and on occasion she would take it out on her only daughter. As Virginia progressed through high school, her relationship with her mother deteriorated. On graduating, she recalls that college never occurred to her; instead she enrolled in the nursing program at the Tri-State Hospital in Shreveport, Louisiana, over the strenuous objections of her mother.

Virginia first met her future husband on a hot midsummer evening in the middle of her shift at the local hospital, and she fell in love with Bill Blythe at first sight. Her feelings were so strong that the next day she called her fiancé to end a four-year relationship.

After a whirlwind courtship that lasted barely two months, Virginia and Bill were married on September 3, 1943. A few weeks after the wedding, Bill was shipped off to the Mediterranean. Virginia would not see her husband again for two years.

By the time Bill Blythe was discharged from the armed forces in November 1945, Virginia had completed her training and was a practicing nurse. Bill had a job waiting for him in Chicago selling heavy construction equipment, so the young couple loaded their belongings into his Buick and drove hundreds of miles to the city to begin their new life together.

Throughout the country millions of returning veterans

were also striking out on their own and in the process creating a severe housing shortage. In Chicago, Bill and Virginia were fortunate to find room in a hotel. As a salesman, Bill was away from home most of the time. Within a few months, when Virginia became pregnant, the couple decided that it would be best if she moved back to Hope to stay with her parents until they could find a house of their own.

In May 1946, Bill bought a small house, and on Friday, May 17, he left work in the afternoon intending to drive to Hope, pick up his young wife, and move his family to a new home near Chicago. He never made it. A tire blew, causing the car to crash into a drainage ditch, and Bill Blythe was knocked unconscious, fell out of the car face down in the water-filled ditch, and drowned. Barely into her twenties, Virginia Blythe was a pregnant widow facing the prospect of providing for her child alone. Three months later, on August 19, 1946, her son was born.

From the moment Virginia brought Billy home to her parents' Hervey Street home, Edith Cassidy struggled to provide a loving home. In a bid to gain financial freedom for herself and her son, Virginia decided to return to school and attain a license as an nurse-anesthetist. The decision was a difficult one: Virginia would have to leave Billy with her mother for two years while she attended school at Charity Hospital in New Orleans.

According to Roger Morris's biography *Partners in Power: The Clintons and Their America*, the memory of that first separation left a deep mark on Clinton, who recalls his mother "crying and actually falling down on her knees by the railbed" and Edith Cassidy comforting him as their train pulled out of New Orleans.

Billy, as everyone called him, was surrounded by love and affection in the Cassidy household. Edith, whom he called "mawmaw," was the dominant figure of his early years. While he was still in diapers she taught her grandson how to read, quizzing him with homemade flash cards as he sat in his high chair. Edith also introduced her young charge to religion at the First Baptist Church. "[My grand-parents] had a lot to do with my early commitment to learning," Clinton was later quoted as saying in *The Come-back Kid: The Life and Career of Bill Clinton*. "They didn't have much formal education, but they really helped [embed] in me a real sense of educational achievement."

Whenever he escaped the watchful eye of his grand-mother, Billy spent most of his days playing in his grand-father's grocery store. It was at the general store that the future president first came into contact with the share-cropping system of agriculture in the South. He watched as his grandfather extended credit to poor farmers, using their future earnings as collateral. Unlike many of the store owners in the racially segregated town of Hope, Arkansas, Eldridge Cassidy gave credit to black and white share-croppers alike. On sunny days young Billy played with the sons of black farmers as their fathers bargained with his grandfather. When it rained he could be found inside lis-tening to his grandfather discuss politics and tell stories.

When Billy was four years old, Virginia Blythe returned to Hope. She also remarried. Bill's new stepfa-ther, Roger Clinton, owned a local car dealership. Unfor-tunately, he was also abusive, an alcoholic, and a gambler, and he sold alcohol and on occasion organized craps or poker games for money—illegal activities in Hempstead County, Arkansas.

In the years that followed, young Billy was often dropped off with his grandparents while Virginia and her new husband went off to the racetrack or casinos in Hot Springs, Arkansas. At home, Billy's bedroom was only separated from his parents' room by a thin wall. As he lay in his bed at night the young boy could hear his mother's screams when Roger beat her. On one occasion, as Vir-ginia and five-year-old Billy were leaving to visit the Cas-sidys, Roger pulled out a gun and fired a bullet into the wall above their heads. Billy watched from the refuge of a neighbor's kitchen as his stepfather was handcuffed and

Bill's mother and grandmother sparked in him a passion for learning of all kinds. In addition to his academic efforts, Bill exercised his musical skills by learning to play the tenor saxophone. Shown here in junior high school, by the time he graduated from Hot Springs High School he had been selected for the state band and played with two other friends in a music group known as The Three Blind Mice.

dragged off to jail by the police. Recalling those painful days, Clinton later noted, "There was a bullet hole in the wall. It could have ricocheted, hit my mother, hit me. . . . I had to live with that bullet hole, look at it every day."

Through his early childhood Bill Clinton remained affable and easygoing. Like many children of abusive and alcoholic parents, he was forced to allow outsiders to see only what he wanted them to see. He never allowed his friends or teachers to know what was occurring behind the closed doors of his house. His bond to his mother grew ever stronger as the abuse continued. When his brother Roger was born, Billy automatically became his protector, inside and outside the home.

When Billy was seven, the family moved from Hope to the larger city of Hot Springs. Billy was enrolled in St. Johns, a parochial school, but by the fourth grade he switched to the Ramble Public School. Unfortunately, the public schools of Arkansas were among the worst in the nation. Many of the teachers were unqualified for the subjects they taught, and the state did not require them to attain a college degree. Virginia Clinton's constant complaints about the poor quality of schools in Arkansas left a lasting impression on her son, who would later make education reform in Arkansas and the United States one of his most important goals.

Bill's stepfather was slowly being consumed by alcoholism, and as he spiraled downward he directed his abuse toward his wife and sons. On several occasions Virginia was forced to flee to a neighbor's house or local motel until her husband's rage subsided. Billy was growing quickly, and by the time he was 14 he was over six feet tall and 200 pounds—big enough, he thought, to stop the continued abuse by his stepfather. Virginia recalled in her autobiography that one night as Roger was beating her, their bedroom door came crashing down. Standing in the hallway was her son Bill. "Daddy," he said, "stand up." Too drunk to rise, Roger could only stare slack-jawed at his stepson, who grabbed him under the arms and lifted him to eye level. "Hear me," he said in a quiet but menacing tone, "Never . . . ever . . . touch my mother again."

Like many women who are caught in an abusive relationship, Virginia sometimes blamed herself for her situation or believed that she could change her husband. When Bill Clinton was in high school, Virginia divorced Roger, but after only 83 days apart they reconciled and quickly remarried.

Bill Clinton blossomed when he entered Hot Springs High School. His fierce determination to succeed, instilled in him by his mother and grandmother, combined with the amiable good nature he had inherited from his birth father,

Being elected the Arkansas senator to the 1963 American Legion Boys' Nation in Washington, D.C., fueled Bill's deep political desire. He is pictured here with his Boys' Nation class (first row, third from right). During the weekend convention, Bill was able to meet his idol, President John F. Kennedy. Later in his life, Bill would recall this handshake as the moment that inspired his political career.

made him a success in the classroom and popular outside of school. Bill soon found that he had a talent for music and became a tenor saxophonist in the high school band. As his playing improved he and two classmates formed a band called The Three Blind Mice. Clinton was also elected president of his class during his sophomore and junior years, a precursor of his career to come.

Hot Springs High School principal Johnnie Mae Mackey fueled young Bill Clinton's interest in politics. Mackey was an influential member of the American Legion and a small cog in Arkansas governor Orval Faubus's political organization. With her backing, Clinton gained entry to Boys' State, a summer camp where Arkansas's best students learned about politics and the electoral process by creating political parties and holding mock elections. At the camp held after Clinton's junior year, he was elected a senator of Boys' State. With other Boys' State senators

from all over the country, he traveled to Washington, D.C., for the Boys' Nation convention in July 1963.

While in the nation's capital, Bill and the other delegates from Arkansas were invited to lunch in the Senate dining room. At the luncheon Bill met Senator J. William Fulbright, an influential Arkansas Democrat who was chairman of the Senate Foreign Relations Committee. Fulbright would one day be Clinton's political mentor.

The highlight of the week was a visit to the White House, where President John F. Kennedy greeted the entire group. Clinton slowly worked his way to the front of the line, and when Kennedy was through with his prepared remarks the 16-year old surged forward and clasped the president's hand.

When Kennedy was felled by an assassin's bullet four months later, Clinton gave an emotional speech about his fallen hero before an American Legion audience in his

Bill's friendly, warm nature made him a favorite in and out of high school. He is shown here at the 1965 Hot Springs Debutante Ball with friend Rosalie Lepeltier.

hometown. The next year he graduated fourth in his class of 323 students. As a senior, Bill was a member of the National Honor Society and was a National Merit Scholarship finalist.

He chose to attend college at Georgetown University's School of Foreign Service for one overriding reason: its location in Washington, D.C. His goal was to combine the practical experience of working for a politician on Capitol Hill with the more regimented course work of the university.

For Bill Clinton, the nation's capital and Georgetown held academic promise, social excitement, and political possibility. Bill was active in student government: he is shown here during a relaxed moment as freshman class president.

3

FROM STUDENT
TO POLITICIAN

WHEN BILL CLINTON entered Georgetown University in 1964, he decided to study international affairs. Tuition was expensive and Clinton always held at least one part-time job to supplement his family's financial support.

It didn't take Bill Clinton long to settle in at Georgetown. His easygoing manner, coupled with his intelligence, charm, and sincerity, soon overcame any inhibitions his more affluent classmates may have felt about the underprivileged boy from one of the poorest states in the country. Recalling those days, Clinton said, "I'd never been out of Arkansas really very much, and there I was with people from all over the country and all over the world." Those people must have liked and trusted the young man, because Clinton was elected president of his freshman and sophomore classes.

College was a busy time for Clinton; in addition to his jobs to help pay tuition, he also worked as a volunteer in a student clinic for alcoholics and still managed to maintain a 3.57 grade point average. He was able to juggle so many activities because he had developed the capacity to sleep only five hours a night, supplemented with a few 20-minute catnaps during the day.

In the summer before his sophomore year Clinton returned to Arkansas as a campaign volunteer for Frank Holt, a Democratic candidate for governor. Although Holt lost the election, Clinton impressed many of the people associated with the campaign, demonstrating his understanding of state politics, ability to give speeches, and indefatigable spirit. The contacts he made also helped him get a part-time position as a member of Senator Fulbright's Washington staff. His enthusiasm at entering the arena to which he intended to devote his life can be seen in an excerpt of a letter that Clinton wrote to his grandmother, which was reprinted in the Pulitzer Prize-winning biography *First in His Class: A Biography of Bill Clinton*:

> I attend class in the morning and at night and work in the afternoon. It is of course exciting to be here around all the senators and already this year I've seen the president [and] the vice president . . . . There's not much time to do anything but study and work, but I love being busy and hard work is good for people.

As an aide to Senator Fulbright, Clinton was able to witness firsthand many of the important political issues of the day. One of these was the role of the United States military in the Southeast Asian nation of Vietnam. Senator Fulbright, the chairman of the Senate Foreign Relations Committee, had been a supporter of the 1964 Gulf of Tonkin Resolution that gave President Lyndon B. Johnson broad congressional approval to wage war against Vietnam, but as American casualties mounted the senator became one of the most vocal opponents of the conflict that was drawing thousands of young Americans into the U.S. military. In 1966 there were 400,000 American soldiers fighting in Vietnam, and most of them had been drafted into the service.

Clinton himself managed to avoid the military draft. He

was granted a college deferment when he entered Georgetown, and when the draft was later changed to a lottery system, Clinton's number was high enough to keep him out of the military. In the future, political opponents would attempt to cast doubt on his draft history, but Clinton has countered, "I certainly had no leverage to get special treatment from the draft board," and said that his high lottery number "was just a fluke."

Another issue tearing at the social fabric of the country during Clinton's time on Fulbright's staff was a continuing struggle by African Americans for equality. After the Supreme Court's 1954 *Brown v. Board of Education* decision nullifying federal tolerance of racial discrimination, black citizens throughout the country fought to eliminate discrimination and segregation. Although President Lyndon B. Johnson had signed the Civil Rights Act of 1964 and the Voting Rights Act of 1965 into law, there continued to be a large difference between the opportunities and living standards afforded black and white Americans.

Although Clinton admired Senator Fulbright's views on most matters, race relations was not one of them. In 1956, Fulbright, along with 18 of his Senate colleagues and 27 southern representatives, had signed the Southern Manifesto, which declared their intention of opposing desegregation in the South.

Dr. Martin Luther King Jr., a young African-American minister, had become one of the primary leaders of the modern civil rights movement, and his call for nonviolent opposition to injustices had gained him a large national

A REALISTIC APPROACH TO STUDENT GOVERNMENT

BILL CLINTON

CANDIDATE

PRESIDENT OF THE STUDENT COUNCIL

A poster from Clinton's campaign for president of the Georgetown Student Council reveals Bill's already well-developed desire for political involvement.

following. After King was assassinated in 1968, angry African Americans rioted in many cities, including Washington, D.C., Clinton volunteered to deliver Red Cross supplies during the riots, and he saw destruction and despair on the streets of the nation's capital that he was never able to forget. At night he would climb to the roof of his dormitory and watch as the city burned around him.

While his proximity to the important policy decisions of the day was exciting, life was not perfect for Bill Clinton. In the midst of his senior year at Georgetown, his stepfather was diagnosed with cancer. Roger Clinton had never reconciled with his stepson, so with Roger's death imminent Bill drove home from Georgetown every weekend for the next six weeks to spent time with his stepfather. As Roger's condition deteriorated, the two finally came to peace with each other. When Roger died, Clinton was at his side. He later told the *New York Times*, "I think he knew that I was coming down there because I loved him. There was nothing else to fight over; nothing else to run from. It was a wonderful time in my life, and I think in his."

After he graduated from Georgetown University in 1968, Clinton was offered a Rhodes scholarship to attend Oxford University in England, one of the world's oldest and most prestigious universities. This educational opportunity gave him a chance to devote himself fully to his academic pursuits. He later told reporter David Broder of the *Washington Post* that "being in England was incredible. I got to travel a lot . . . learn things, go see things . . . it was a great deal."

Clinton took full advantage of his time at Oxford by auditing lectures on subjects outside of his field of politics and economics, traveling throughout Europe and the Soviet Union, and reading as many books as possible. He later estimated that he read about 300 books in the two years that he attended Oxford.

After two years, however, Clinton decided to return to school in the United States. Although he still had a year to

go on his Rhodes scholarship, he realized that a law degree was essential in order to pursue a political career, so he applied to the law school at Yale University. He also feared that he might be missing political opportunities in Washington and Arkansas. At Yale, Clinton could test himself against some of the best legal minds in the country and add to his growing network of friends.

Clinton entered Yale's law school in the fall of 1971. However, even though he had a full scholarship, he also held various part-time jobs to make ends meet. He taught at a local community college, investigated civil suits for a New Haven law firm, and worked briefly for a local city councilman. His duties as an investigator took him to the slums of New Haven, Connecticut, where he witnessed the growing despair of those trapped in the inner city.

Although Yale was one of the best law schools in the country, Clinton had little difficulty with his course work. Friends recall how he could miss lectures but borrow their notes and prepare for his exams by studying the night

After Martin Luther King's assassination in 1968, rioting broke out in cities across the country. Clinton worked as a Red Cross volunteer during the riots in Washington, D.C., pictured above.

before they were scheduled.

During his first year at Yale, Clinton met an intelligent, industrious woman named Hillary Rodham. At first glance, Bill Clinton and Hillary Rodham seemed like opposites. While he had lived in near-poverty, she had grown up in the wealthy Chicago suburb of Park Ridge. But like Clinton, Hillary was driven to achieve. Hillary had been a National Merit Scholarship finalist and a member of the National Honor Society in high school. At prestigious Wellesley College in Massachusetts she became a student activist, fighting for the elimination of racial and gender discrimination. In 1968 she worked for the presidential campaign of Minnesota senator Eugene McCarthy. As a student of politics, Hillary was drawn to Washington, and during her senior year at Wellesley she won an internship with Illinois congressman Harold Collier. The internship solidified her desire to become active in public policy.

Bill and Hillary were in many of the same law classes at Yale, but had never been formally introduced. Clinton recalls following her after class trying to work up the courage to introduce himself. Finally, after Hillary found him gazing at her in the law library, she approached and said, "Look, if you're going to keep staring at me and I'm going to be staring back, I think we should at least know each other." She then reached out her hand, saying, "I'm Hillary Rodham. What's your name?" Clinton was surprised by her straightforward nature and almost forgot his own name as he answered her. Soon the pair were inseparable.

In 1972 Hillary and Bill took time off from their legal studies and went to Texas to work on the presidential campaign of Senator George McGovern of South Dakota. McGovern's campaign was built around one theme: ending American involvement in Vietnam.

Four years earlier, Richard Nixon had gained the presidency in large part because he promised that he would end the war. In his four years as America's chief executive,

Life wasn't all studies for Bill Clinton during his years as a Yale law student. During his first year at the law school, he met Hillary Rodham, pictured here during her student days. The two quickly developed a serious relationship.

Nixon had only succeeded in spreading the war to the neighboring countries of Laos and Cambodia. Bill and Hillary were among thousands of college students from across the country who joined the McGovern campaign. The 1972 presidential race came to symbolize the growing rift between what Nixon called the "silent majority" of middle Americans who supported him, and the "baby boomers"—the generation born after World War II.

Clinton's work on the McGovern campaign laid the groundwork for his future political success in Arkansas. Although Clinton had worked on other election campaigns, the work he did during this presidential race gave him stature in Democratic Party politics in his home state. During the campaign Bill Clinton returned to Little Rock as an emissary of the party's presidential candidate and dealt with the political leaders of Arkansas as a peer. He told the *Arkansas Gazette*, "I was asked to come to Arkansas to make as many friends as I could." Reporters noted Clinton's past successes at Hot Springs High School

Both Bill and Hillary took time off from Yale Law School to aid Senator George McGovern's presidential campaign in 1972. Though McGovern lost the election, Bill's work was central to the Democratic candidate's campaign in Arkansas. In this picture (left to right), Clinton, McGovern, and Joe Purcell, chairman of the state Democratic party, confer in Little Rock.

and his years at Oxford and predicted "a bright future" for this "prodigal son of Arkansas." While Clinton was traveling or coordinating activities at the campaign headquarters in Austin, Hillary was canvassing the poor neighborhoods of San Antonio, Texas, registering new voters.

Because of his hard work, Clinton was offered a chance to be the coordinator for the Arkansas delegation to the Democratic National Convention, which would be held in Miami during July. McGovern was selected as the Democratic candidate during the convention. However, Clinton and other insiders knew that he did not have broad enough support to win the presidential election against the incumbent, Nixon. Years later Clinton told a reporter, "This campaign and this man did not have a core, a center, that was common to a great majority of the country." On election night in November 1972 President Nixon was reelected by one of the largest electoral margins in American history.

Following the campaign, Bill and Hillary returned to Yale together. After they graduated in 1973, they were confronted with a dilemma that many professional couples face: whose career would take precedence? Clinton had always made it clear that he intended to return to Arkansas and pursue a political career, and he wanted Hillary to join him and become his wife. However, there were few opportunities in Arkansas for a woman with Hillary's training or beliefs, and if she chose to marry Clinton she faced the prospect of setting her own career aside.

Uncertain what path she wanted her career to follow, Hillary Rodham accepted a position as a staff counsel for the House of Representatives' Judiciary Committee. This committee was conducting an inquiry into the role of top members of the Nixon administration in an illegal campaign of sabotage against the Democratic National Committee (DNC) before the 1972 election, including a failed burglary and bugging attempt at the DNC's headquarters in the Watergate Hotel in Washington, D.C.

Bill Clinton was also offered a position on the Judiciary Committee, but he declined. Instead, he decided to return home to Arkansas.

Dale Bumpers, a popular Arkansas senator, supported 28-year-old Bill Clinton in his first campaign for public office, a 1974 bid to represent Arkansas's Third District in the House of Representatives.

4

ENTERING ARKANSAS POLITICS

AFTER GRADUATING FROM YALE, Clinton obtained a teaching position at the University of Arkansas School of Law located in Fayetteville, a small college community in the Ozark Mountains near the Missouri border. In applying for the teaching post, Clinton had to overcome an obstacle that he could do nothing about: his youth. Because he was only 27 years old and fresh out of law school, many on the faculty considered Clinton's age and lack of experience in practicing law an impediment. Clinton countered this by arguing, "I've been too young to do everything I've ever done," and impressed the faculty so much in his initial interview that they voted unanimously for his appointment.

Although he could have earned a much higher salary by accepting any one of several job offers with Washington law firms, the teaching position was an excellent way for Clinton to begin his his political career in Arkansas. Many of his students were the future business and political leaders of Arkansas, and after being introduced to Clinton, more than a few became lifelong friends and political allies. With his long curly hair and a seemingly casual approach to his classes, Clinton soon became a favorite among first-year students. He was an easy grader and could often be found in the student cafeteria discussing politics. Years later, many recalled how easily Clinton was able to relate current events to the study of law, paying particular attention to the travails of President Nixon and the growing Watergate scandals in Washington, and the debate over abortion, women's rights, and other issues. The faculty of the law school was entirely white, and Clinton soon became a mentor to the few black students accepted into the program. It was common to find a group of these students sitting around his kitchen table at night and on weekends, discussing court cases and cramming for exams.

Although he found his teaching duties challenging and interesting, Clinton yearned to be part of the political process in Arkansas. After all, that was the reason he had left Washington, D.C., and turned down lucrative job offers from prestigious law firms. He was determined to improve the life of the average citizen of his home state. He realized that with his outstanding educational achievements he had the potential to be one of the political leaders of his generation, much like his idol, John F. Kennedy.

Within months of returning to Arkansas, Clinton decided to seek election to the U.S. House of Representatives. If he succeeded in capturing the House seat he would have the best of both worlds: a political life in Washington representing the interests of his home state, and, just as important, he would be reunited with Hillary Rodham, who was living and working in the nation's capital. Surrounded by his family and friends, Bill Clinton announced his candidacy for the House of Representatives on February 25, 1974.

The Third Congressional District, which Clinton was seeking to represent, included his hometown of Hot Springs, his new residence in Fayetteville, and a large rural area of small communities stretching across northwest Arkansas. In order to win the election Clinton would have to canvass the entire district and meet personally with the voters.

At an early age, Clinton had started filling out index cards about the people he met during his travels. He would note the circumstances of his meeting, the person's political beliefs, books they had discussed, and any friends or relatives they had in common. The cards, which now numbered in the thousands, paid off by providing Clinton's initial base of support. After reviewing the cards, he called on family, friends, former classmates and students, reporters, political operatives from his days on the McGovern campaign, professors from Oxford and Georgetown, and, most important of all, the hundreds of young Arkansans that he had gone to high school with, competed against in band competitions, or met through Boys' State.

The response was immediate. Envelopes began arriving at Clinton's Fayetteville home and his mother's house in Hot Springs with checks for $10, $20, or $50 contributions. Also, some friends put their careers on hold and moved to Arkansas temporarily to help with the campaign.

Clinton's first campaign was a grassroots, family affair. Bill's mother Virginia worked the phones ceaselessly, and together with some of his high school friends sat at her kitchen table calling friends and strangers alike, soliciting contributions and volunteers. Bill's uncle Raymond pitched in with a $10,000 donation and offered use of a house in Hot Springs that soon became Clinton's campaign headquarters. Virginia made thousands of "Clinton for Congress" signs and proudly plastered them on her car, on telephone poles, and along streets throughout Hot Springs.

The campaign was a learning experience for Clinton, who recalls, "I just got in my little car and drove and had a hell of a time." The sight of Clinton arriving in town in his cramped and dented 1970 Gremlin reminded many voters that for all his intellectual accomplishments, he

In his 1974 congressional campaign, Clinton challenged Republican incumbent John Hammerschmidt, a Nixon supporter who was very popular with his constituency.

was still one of them. The Gremlin was eventually replaced with a used pickup truck that Clinton drove to all corners of his district.

Arriving in a town or hamlet, Clinton first sought the general store, where he was always sure to find a small group of potential voters. Familiar with this unique small-town institution from his youth behind his grandfather's store counter, Clinton would greet these strangers, and before long he would be on a first-name basis with many of them. From there he was off to the courthouse, where he would find the local peace officer or county judge whose endorsement he needed. As he visited the small villages, Clinton would often be invited to speak about political issues, like legislation that would affect the local community, President Nixon's policies concerning Vietnam, or the growing Watergate scandal. Clinton was at his best during these impromptu talks, and as he looked his fellow Arkansans in the eyes he impressed them with his knowledge and common sense.

When no candidate won a majority in the Democratic primary, Clinton was forced to campaign in a runoff with his closest rival. He won easily, capturing 69 percent of the vote to become the Democratic candidate for the general election.

Clinton would be facing a formidable opponent in the November election: popular incumbent John Paul Hammerschmidt. Hammerschmidt, a Republican, had first been elected in 1966 and in each succeeding contest had added to his electoral victories; in 1972 he had received 77 percent of the vote. Hammerschmidt's constituent service and his position on the House Veterans' Committee made him popular with older voters. He had been a fighter pilot during World War II and was a staunch supporter of President Nixon's policies in Vietnam.

As the Clinton campaign swung into high gear during the summer of 1974, Hillary Rodham moved to Fayetteville to help out. She had already taken the Arkansas bar

During his bid for the House of Representatives in 1974, Clinton hammered his popular Republican opponent about his support of President Nixon during the Watergate scandal. Clinton's opposition to the war in Vietnam also drew support.

exam, which lawyers must pass in order to practice law in the state, and she accepted a position on the law school faculty. She also threw her considerable energy and talent for organization into Bill's campaign. Although Bill Clinton was good with people, he was not very organized and would often schedule two or more appearances for the same time. Hillary brought order and discipline to the campaign. Before long, her father and two brothers joined her in Arkansas to help. They answered phones at campaign headquarters, solicited donations, served as drivers for Clinton, and did anything else necessary to help Bill and Hillary succeed.

In her memoirs, Virginia Kelley recalled her son's passion for Hillary. On a trip home to Hot Springs just before leaving Yale he had taken her aside and said, "Mother, I want you to pray for me. Pray that it's Hillary. Because I'll tell you this: for me it's Hillary or it's nobody."

In 1974, as evidence grew that Nixon had been involved in the Watergate scandal, many representatives, both Democrats and Republicans, called for his impeachment. On the campaign trail, Clinton continually attacked Hammerschmidt for his support of the beleaguered president, and voters who believed that Nixon was involved in the Watergate scandal switched their support to the young Democrat. When Nixon relinquished his office on August 9, 1974, becoming the only president in American history to resign in disgrace, Clinton lost his most potent weapon against Hammerschmidt as the country's attention turned to other matters.

Another important campaign issue was the continued presence of American combat troops in Vietnam. The war in Southeast Asia had divided the nation, leading to demonstrations in the streets of many major American cities. College students on campuses throughout the country held peace marches and clashed with authorities. Clinton opposed the war, believing that the conflict in Vietnam was an internal civil war in which the United States should play no part. Arkansas voters who opposed Hammerschmidt's position on the war and wanted the United States to pull its troops out of Vietnam gave their support to Clinton.

Clinton represented a new generation that had come of age during the Vietnam conflict. By questioning authority, seeking new ways to solve the growing inequities in American society, and speaking out against racial and economic injustice, Clinton hoped to build a bridge between his own generation and the one that had come of age during the Great Depression and World War II.

On the eve of the election, the candidates were nearly even in public opinion polls. When the votes were finally counted, Hammerschmidt had narrowly defeated Clinton, capturing slightly over 51 percent of the vote.

Although he lost the election, Clinton realized that his campaign had been a success. He had gained valuable experience, proven that he had a natural knack for campaigning, become known throughout the state, and, most important, convinced Hillary Rodham to move to Arkansas. He later told reporters that "it was the best campaign I ever ran." By losing his bid to go to Washington. Clinton would begin his political service at the state level rather than in federal government.

Ambitious, idealistic, and undaunted by his failed congressional campaign, Bill Clinton set his sights on state politics in 1976, when he ran for the state's highest law-enforcement position, attorney general.

5

VICTORY
AND DEFEAT

BILL CLINTON RETURNED to his teaching duties at the University of Arkansas School of Law following his defeat for the House of Representatives. However, his political ambition had not waned, and he believed that he could start formulating the progressive programs and policies necessary to raise the dismal living standards in Arkansas. During the summer and fall of 1975 Clinton began building a statewide political organization that would help him in his next election.

Hillary Rodham continued teaching at the University of Arkansas and became involved in community work in her adopted state. She was named director of the University of Arkansas Law Clinic and recruited law students to volunteer their time and energy to help indigent clients. In her role as director, she petitioned judges, legislators, and the state's leading attorneys to endorse the clinic's goals. She also established progressive inmate-rights programs at several Arkansas penitentiaries.

In the summer of 1975 Bill surprised Hillary by purchasing a small red-brick cottage near the university and proposing marriage. She happily accepted his proposal.

Hillary Rodham had decided that her future lay with Bill Clinton. She believed that he had the potential to make a real difference in American society, and years later she told a journalist, "I just knew I wanted to be part of a changing world."

Bill and Hillary were married on October 11, 1975, in the living room of their modest new home. The wedding was a private affair, with only immediate family and a few close friends attending the service. Bill's brother Roger served as his best man, and the simple ceremony was performed by Victor Nixon, a Methodist minister who had befriended Clinton during his race for the House of Representatives.

As a feminist who had come of age during the 1960s, Hillary was not willing to change her name; she retained the name Rodham. She had, after all, moved to Arkansas, sacrificing her own promising Washington career for marriage to Bill Clinton. The retention of her family name represented both her individual identity and her independence. Her new husband understood and supported her decision.

According to *Partners in Power*, Hillary told close friends that she intended to be "a person in my own right" and not a mere appendage of her husband. Hillary's political role model was former first lady Eleanor Roosevelt, who had carved out a political niche of her own while her husband, Franklin Delano Roosevelt, was serving as governor of New York State and president of the United States. Eleanor Roosevelt eventually became a syndicated columnist, a champion of civil rights and women's rights, and a Democratic Party power broker.

In 1976, Bill Clinton decided to run in his second election, as a candidate for attorney general of Arkansas. The incumbent attorney general, Jim Guy Tucker, was giving up the position so that he could run for Congress. The position of attorney general, the top law-enforcement official in the state, was considered a natural stepping-stone to the governorship.

Traditionally, Arkansas voters were mostly Democrats; if Clinton prevailed in the Democratic Party primary, he was likely to win the general election. The Democratic primary was a three-man race, with Clinton facing Arkansas secretary of state George Jernigan and deputy attorney general Clarence Cash. Although both of his opponents had more experience in state government, Clinton had an advantage: the tightly knit political organization he had developed. Dubbing his campaign a "crusade," he asked friends and contacts for their support in the election.

His supporters did not disappoint him; he received over 60 percent of the vote in the Democratic primary, carrying all but a handful of rural counties.

Clinton shared the Democratic Party ticket with Governor David Pryor, who had first been elected to the Arkansas state house in 1974 and after a two-year term was still quite popular with the state electorate. Clinton's support was so strong that the Republican Party did not put a candidate forward to oppose him in the general election.

Nationally, another southern Democrat was making a bid for the presidency in 1976. Following the Watergate scandal and resignation of President Nixon, many Americans wanted a president who was not a Washington "insider." Former Georgia governor Jimmy Carter hoped to be that man. His running mate was Minnesota senator Walter Mondale. Gerald Ford, who had become president after Nixon resigned in 1974, was attempting to win a four-year term of his own with Senator Robert Dole as his vice-presidential nominee.

With his own election all but assured, Clinton took on the added task of managing Carter's presidential campaign in Arkansas. Clinton worked 18 hours a day giving speeches at county fairs, meeting people at rural courthouses, and doing whatever else was necessary to get both himself and the national Democratic candidates elected.

It was an ideal position for Clinton. If Carter gained the presidency, Clinton would be among the most important

Clinton is shown here in a casual meeting during his 1976 campaign for attorney general. The base of support Bill had worked to build in Arkansas during his run for Congress two years earlier helped him to easily win the election.

Democrats in the state. Also, a grateful Carter could one day help Clinton, who had already decided to seek the governorship of Arkansas in 1978. As the manager of Carter's Arkansas operation, Clinton was able to make important connections with national Democratic leaders and renew old friendships from his days as a McGovern campaign volunteer. As the official representative of the Democratic presidential nominee, Clinton's views and opinions were given much more credence than those of a mere candidate for state office. His position also gained him access to the inner circles of the national Democratic Party. These ties would prove crucial to Clinton as he moved from the state to the national political arena.

Hillary Rodham took a leave of absence from her law school duties to manage Carter's Indiana campaign effort, and her adept management style earned the gratitude of many national Democratic leaders.

Fueled in part by anti-Republican sentiment caused by the Watergate scandal, Carter narrowly won the election, with 50 percent of the vote to Ford's 48 percent. In Arkansas, David Pryor and Bill Clinton easily won office, and in January 1977, Clinton was sworn in as attorney general of Arkansas.

Jimmy Carter thanked Clinton for his help in securing Arkansas's four electoral votes, and he named Hillary Rodham to the National Board of Legal Services Corporation in thanks for her efforts in Indiana. She soon rose to the presidency of the organization.

During his two-year tenure as Arkansas attorney general, Clinton managed to reduce overcrowding in the state's penitentiaries by establishing a statewide work-release program for nonviolent offenders. Clinton was an activist attorney general, who, as the state's public advocate, often appeared unannounced at public hearings throughout the state to represent the citizens' interests. He also established new government agencies to help consumers fight fraud, oversee utility and telephone companies, and promote energy conservation.

Following his first year in office, Clinton published and distributed the *Attorney General's Report*, the first for an Arkansas attorney general, in which he recounted all the activities of his office.

In 1978 Governor Pryor decided not to seek a third term; instead, he chose to run for the United States Senate. Upon hearing Pryor's announcement, Clinton immediately announced that he would be a candidate for the vacant governor's position. He easily swept the Democratic primary with over 60 percent of the vote, and in the general election he overwhelmingly defeated Republican nominee Lynn Lowe to become, at age 32, the youngest governor in the United States in almost half a century. He later told reporters that running for governor was "a little bit like running for class president."

Because of his overwhelming support in the election, Clinton felt he had a mandate for change from the people of Arkansas, and he intended to be the most progressive governor in the state's history. He quickly set the two priorities of his administration: education and health reform.

Soon after taking office he commissioned his wife, Hillary, to form a state task force to examine the condition of rural health care and ways to improve it. The task force soon implemented a network of small health clinics in rural areas where there were no doctors.

Governor Clinton's top priority was education, and his administration drafted legislation to improve the conditions of the public school system and raise the pay of the state's public school teachers. Having benefited from the best education that America and England could offer, Clinton firmly believed that education was the strongest weapon against poverty. His legislative program included a plan to test all Arkansas teachers in the subjects they taught.

In his January 15, 1979, "State of the State" address, Clinton outlined his reform plan, which included a bill that would make it harder to dismiss teachers without cause, a requirement that new teachers pass a standard competency exam before being licensed to teach in Arkansas, and mandatory achievement tests for all students in third, sixth, and eighth grades each year. Clinton also suggested that the state Board of Education should consider consolidating school districts to eliminate over six million dollars in state subsidies given to smaller districts.

The school consolidation issue was a hot topic, as the residents of rural communities felt that closing their local schools and busing students to a regional school would destroy their towns' identities. The proposed bill caused so much controversy that Clinton was forced to withdraw the legislation—his first major political defeat.

Other aspects of his education reform were more accepted. His "Fair Dismissal Bill," which protected Arkansas teachers from termination for "arbitrary, capricious, and unsubstantiated reasons," was passed, as was a bill that raised teacher salaries throughout the state. In all, he increased funding for public education to 40 percent of the Arkansas budget.

In order to pay for these new initiatives, Governor Clinton proposed raising gasoline taxes and licensing fees for car and truck registrations. He hoped the burden of the new taxes would fall mainly on Arkansas's large trucking and poultry industries because he felt they could better absorb the increase. However, the state legislature refused to raise industrial fees, and most of the new tax burden fell on ordinary citizens, which caused dissatisfaction among the electorate.

Bill is sworn in as governor of Arkansas, with wife Hillary Rodham by his side. When Clinton was elected in 1978, at age 32, he was the youngest governor in the United States.

As governor, Bill Clinton proposed ambitious legislation; however, his popularity waned as a result of taxes passed to pay for new programs, as well as outside events that affected Arkansas, such as the settlement of Cuban refugees at Fort Chaffee.

And not everyone was happy with the new initiatives themselves. The standards he set for educational reform were met with fierce opposition from teachers' unions; teachers resented and feared the prospect of losing their positions because Clinton wanted all teachers, not just new ones, to take a competency test. Also, his network of health-care clinics proved to be unpopular with doctors and health-care professionals, who often clashed with social workers at the clinics over responsibilities.

One bright spot during Bill and Hillary's first two years in the Arkansas governor's mansion was the birth of their daughter, Chelsea Victoria Clinton, on February 27, 1980. The Clintons doted on their only child. However, her birth might have been the last good thing to happen to Bill Clinton during 1980, as his political popularity dropped.

Although there was dissatisfaction with the new taxes that had been levied to pay for education and health reforms, an international incident also affected Arkansas, and Bill Clinton's chances for reelection, in 1979. After Cuban leader Fidel Castro allowed thousands of people to flee his Communist-controlled country and come to the United States, releasing prisoners from jails and asylums to join legitimate political refugees, President Carter announced that he would detain Cuban refugees at Fort Chaffee in northwest Arkansas. Within weeks there were more than 20,000 Cuban refugees living in Fort Chaffee's cramped quarters. When the poor living conditions led to riots, thousands of Cuban refugees streamed through the Arkansas countryside and quickly overwhelmed state troopers and local police.

Clinton was forced to call up the Arkansas National Guard to restore order. Although he was praised for his decisive action, the riots and his unwillingness to refuse Carter's resettlement plan had hurt him politically.

Even though Clinton had maintained his relationship with President Carter, the incumbent president could offer little support in the 1980 election because he was in a tough race for his own political position. During Carter's four-year administration, the country had been plagued by a lagging economy that caused inflation and high unemployment. Although Carter had been successful in some foreign policy matters, especially brokering a peace agreement between longtime enemies Israel and Egypt, his chances for reelection were badly damaged when the American Embassy in Iran was taken over by terrorists who held 52 diplomats hostage for over a year. The troubles at home and abroad helped the Republican challenger, California governor Ronald Reagan, pull ahead of Carter in the polls.

Clinton's opponent in the 1980 Arkansas gubernatorial campaign was Republican Frank White, a Naval Academy graduate and successful businessman. White accused the governor of being out of touch with ordinary voters, and he told voters that Clinton's policies had raised the taxes of the poor and middle class. In appearances across the state, White portrayed Clinton and his "long-haired advisors" as too liberal and too young to run Arkansas. White also attacked Hillary Rodham for being too independent and chastised Arkansas's first lady for not taking her husband's last name.

The year 1980 proved to belong to the Republicans. Clinton was defeated in the polls by White, who was only the second Republican in 100 years to become Arkansas's governor. Clinton later told reporters that he had lost the election because of the refugee riots in Fort Chaffee, his tax plan that had disproportionately affected the poor and middle class, and most important, the perception among a majority of voters that Bill Clinton was too young and inexperienced for the job of governor.

Bill Clinton's political career seemed to have reached its zenith. He had lost the highest elected state office, and the other positions at that level, Arkansas's two senate seats, were held by members of his own party. David Pryor still had four years left in his senate term, and Dale

Bumpers had just been elected to a six-year term with over 60 percent of the vote.

Although his plans were unfinished, Bill Clinton had accomplished a great deal in his two-year term as governor. He established health clinics in the rural parts of the state where local doctors were not available, increased teacher's salaries, instituted standardized tests for both students and for new teachers, and expanded kindergarten and special education programs throughout the entire state. The *Arkansas Gazette* called Clinton's educational incentives his "finest achievement and his greatest unfulfillment."

Bill and Hillary share a tense moment as they watch the election returns in 1980. Although he was defeated, Clinton accomplished a great deal during his two-year term as governor.

Bill jumped back into politics in 1982 when he sought reelection to the governorship. A powerful theme of his campaign was "correcting mistakes."

6

RENEWAL
AND REBIRTH

BILL CLINTON WAS stunned by his second electoral defeat and feared that at the relatively young age of 35 his political career was waning. He had turned his first political defeat, for the House of Representatives in 1974, into a learning experience which had helped him prepare for higher office. With his rejection from the state's highest elective office, Clinton was forced, for the first time in his life, to contemplate a career outside of the political arena.

Hillary Rodham later told a journalist that during this period Bill Clinton thought constantly about his father's early death and unrealized expectations. According to Hillary, Bill "was reading everything he could read, talking to everybody he could talk to, staying up all night, because life was passing him by." Following Frank White's inauguration, Clinton took a position with Wright, Lindsey, and Jennings, a prestigious Little Rock law firm. He also began preparing for a political comeback.

Upon taking his oath of office, Governor White immediately began dismantling the state agencies that Clinton had helped establish during his term as governor. The new governor slashed state funding for special education and kindergarten programs, abolished a division of the energy department, dismissed utility watchdogs, and dismantled local job-training programs. Homemade bumper stickers soon began appearing on cars throughout the state bearing the slogan, "Don't Blame Me—I Voted for Clinton."

It seemed to Bill Clinton that Governor White was determined to turn back time. He had termed his triumph over Clinton as "a victory for the Lord," and in early 1981 the Republican governor sponsored the Creation Science Act. The law required all public schools in the state to teach that man was created as described in the Bible's Book of Genesis, rather than by evolution. This was a belief that followers had labeled "creation science."

The debate over teaching evolution in public schools had raged in Arkansas for over half a century. In 1968 the United States Supreme Court overturned an Arkansas law that prohibited the teaching of any theory that conflicted with the biblical account of creation. In keeping with this earlier ruling, in 1982 federal courts ruled that Governor White's new law was unconstitutional. The governor's defense of creation science made national news and he appeared on network television to defend his stance.

Like most progressive thinkers, Clinton was dismayed by Governor White's regressive political philosophy. It reminded Clinton of former Arkansas governor Orval Faubus's battle against school integration in the 1950s that had done so much damage to the state's national reputation. Bill Clinton had dedicated much of his life to changing the image of Arkansas, and he decided to seek the governorship again and lead the state into the future.

In early February 1982, Clinton declared that he would seek the Democratic Party nomination for governor. In a 30-second television advertisement, he admitted that he had made some mistakes during his first term and asked Arkansas's citizens for their forgiveness and support in the

Bill and Hillary at church. The early 1980s was a time of spiritual regrouping for the Clintons.

future. His televised remarks were unique in Arkansas politics, and his message resonated with the average voter.

Redemption was a powerful theme in Clinton's 1982 campaign. Throughout the campaign Clinton told countless audiences that "you can't lead without listening" and promised voters that he would be more attuned to their wants and needs if elected to a second term. "I made a young man's mistakes," he told reporters. "I had an agenda a mile long, and was so busy doing what I wanted to do I didn't have time to correct mistakes."

To drive the point home that he was truly interested in listening to the concerns of the average voter, Clinton began appearing at town meetings throughout the state. The format suited him perfectly; the casual nature of these meetings allowed his intelligence and dedication to come to the surface.

Clinton always had the capacity to learn from his mistakes, and as the campaign progressed he realized that, although he had a multitude of plans and programs that he knew would be good for his state, he first had to educate the electorate and create a demand for change. He would introduce the town meeting format to national politics in 1992 when he sought the presidency.

Aware that some of the more conservative elements of the electorate resented her independence, and that it was costing her husband votes, Hillary Rodham decided to take Clinton as her last name. In order to help her husband's career, Hillary also softened her image. She traded her glasses for contact lenses, began wearing attractive dresses, and had her hair styled to look more feminine. Despite her new look, Hillary Rodham Clinton still impressed everyone who met her with her intelligence and passion on issues such as education and child care. That fall, the *Arkansas Gazette* described the "new" Hillary favorably: "Mrs. Clinton is almost certainly the best speaker among politician's wives, probably the only one who can fully engage an audience on her own merits, rather than just as somebody else's wife. . . . she has become a good hand-shaking campaigner in the traditional Arkansas style."

Hillary had no interest in concealing her intelligence, and at one candidate's forum she appeared in her husband's stead. After Governor White had finished attacking Clinton's tenure as governor, Hillary stepped briskly up to the podium, looked out at the departing governor and declared in a loud voice, "Frank White, I hope you're out there to hear this." She then refuted all of the governor's attacks on her husband. Aware of Hillary's excellent debating skills, White quickly left the hall before he was forced to rebut her charges.

Clinton capped off his remarkable political comeback by defeating White in the general election, capturing almost 55 percent of the vote. He became the first governor in Arkansas history to recapture the position after being defeated. In an emotional speech following his victory, he told his supporters, "I will look back on this election with a mixture of disbelief that it happened and with a profound sense of humility and gratitude for people like you who worked their hearts out and went the extra mile to do something that no rational person thought could be done."

On January 11, 1983, William Jefferson Clinton was sworn in as governor of Arkansas. In his inaugural address he stated that education reform would be the heart of his legislative agenda. "Over the long run, education is the key to our economic revival and our perennial request for prosperity," Clinton declared. He called for an increase in teachers' salaries, the expansion of educational opportunities in poor and small school districts, and the strengthening of educational requirements in all public schools. "Without competence in basic skills," he warned, "our people cannot move on to more advanced achievement."

Clinton immediately pressured the legislature to establish an Educational Standards Commission to study the state's educational structure and come up with a reform plan to overhaul the system. He then appointed the person he trusted most in the world to chair the commission: Hillary Rodham Clinton. His decision to select his wife to head the commission was a signal to the electorate that the administration would be a collaborative effort. Upon appointing Hillary, Clinton told reporters, "This guarantees that I will have a person who is closer to me than anyone else overseeing the project that is more important to me than anything else."

As head of the commission, Hillary attended public

There was much to celebrate as Clinton reclaimed the governor's seat in 1982. He was the first Arkansas governor ever to win back his position after a defeat, and he viewed his reelection as an opportunity to continue the programs he had started during his first term.

hearings in all of the state's 75 counties to promote the education agenda. She met with countless parents and teachers to discuss how the system could be overhauled and improved upon. When the study was completed, the commission recommended the establishment of new course requirements, a pay raise for all educators, an extended school year, and a qualifying test for all teachers. Hillary told reporters, "We Arkansans have to quit making excuses and accept instead the challenge of excellence for all. . . . If we don't seize the opportunity we have now, we will go backward."

Clinton's education reform program was vehemently opposed by the Arkansas Education Association, which represented the state's public school teachers. Teachers had previously been among Clinton's strongest supporters, but they resented the inclusion of competency tests in the education bill. However, the public was overwhelmingly in favor of teacher testing. Clinton told legislators and teachers alike that the tests were "a small price to pay for the biggest tax increase for education in the history of the state," and he predicted that the tests would "restore the teaching profession to the position of public esteem that I think it deserves."

In October 1983, Governor Clinton called a special session of the state legislature in order to hold a vote on his education agenda. The debate over educational reform was bitter and acrimonious. At the end of the first week of hearings, Clinton told reporters, "This is more important to me personally than whatever political consequences will come of it. . . . It's something that's worth putting myself and whatever career I might have on the line for." After six weeks of grueling debate, with Clinton using all of his persuasive powers, the legislature, by one vote, passed a sales tax increase of one percent that would fund the reform package.

The passage of education reforms was the highlight of Clinton's second term. But in the midst of his success, a problem that afflicted millions of Americans hit home for the Clintons when Bill's younger brother, Roger, was arrested on drug charges by the Arkansas state police in the summer of 1984. Nationwide, an unprecedented epidemic of drug use was occurring in the late 1970s and '80s.

Clinton had been informed by the state police that investigators had videotaped Roger Clinton dealing cocaine. The governor ordered them to continue their investigation, and he awaited the final results. When Roger was arrested, Clinton held a press conference and told the people of Arkansas that drugs were "a curse which has reached epidemic proportions and has plagued the lives of millions of families in our nation, including many in our state." Roger Clinton pleaded guilty and was sentenced to three years in a federal prison; he was paroled in a little over a year.

As 1984 was an election year, Clinton's opponents attempted to use his brother's drug conviction against him. However, many families identified with their governor's plight, and Clinton easily won election to a third term. He received 64 percent of the vote to defeat Republican nominee Woody Freeman.

Despite his family difficulties, 1984 was also the year Clinton became prominent in national Democratic Party politics. He was invited to give a speech at the Democratic National Convention, which was meeting in San Francisco during the summer to choose the Democratic candidates for president and vice president. This was the first time that many Democrats would see and hear the man that magazines like *Time* and *Newsweek* had touted as an emerging moderate in the party. In his speech to the delegates Clinton revealed the direction in which he wanted to take the Democratic Party.

Clinton believed that in order for the Democratic Party to remain the majority party, it had to change with the times. The New Deal coalition begun by President Roosevelt and later consolidated by President Harry S. Truman's Fair Deal policies was almost 50 years old. Clinton believed that his party was tied too strongly to the past and needed to look more to the present and future to solve the problems of society.

"Harry Truman would tell us to forget about 1948 and stand for what Americans think in 1984," Clinton told the delegates. The young Arkansas governor said that only by changing with the times could the Democratic Party hope to "attract the millions of Americans who feel locked out

and won't vote because they think we're irrelevant." He ended his speech with a plea for education reform and challenged his listeners, "What are we going to do about it?"

Back at home in Arkansas, Bill and Hillary had to continually guard against attacks on their education agenda, because the teachers' unions were still battling the state competency tests. Hillary told supporters that she was determined to make sure that her husband's policies were implemented before she took on any added responsibilities, and Bill Clinton stated, "Our education program has a simple goal: to retain the progress of the special session on education and build on it." In March of 1985, he was finally victorious when, after the state court ruled his test constitutional, more than 25,000 teachers took the new competency exam. By 1987, as the reforms took hold, student

After his brother Roger (left) was arrested on drug charges in 1984, Bill Clinton spoke out against rising drug abuse. The public showed their support for Bill by electing him to a third term as governor.

Bill and six-year-old Chelsea Clinton leave a voting booth during Bill's 1986 campaign for governor. Shown here during the Democratic primary, Clinton comfortably won the governor's seat again, with 64 percent of the vote.

performance improved. Scores on standardized tests were up, and the percentage of graduating seniors who moved on to college increased from 38 to 50 percent.

In 1986 Clinton ran for a fourth term, knowing that if he won this election he would be in office for four years, because the state legislature had changed the law to allow governors to serve four-year terms instead of the previous two-year terms.

In the Democratic primary, former Arkansas governor Orval Faubus came out of retirement to challenge Clinton. Faubus, an avowed segregationist who had served six terms as governor, believed that Clinton's policies were far too liberal. However, the electorate liked the direction in which their state was headed, and Clinton soundly defeated Faubus in the primary.

In the general election, he faced a familiar opponent: Frank White, the former Republican governor who had defeated Clinton in 1980. As in the primary, Arkansas's voters chose to look forward with their young, progressive governor. Clinton received 64 percent of the vote in the general election to easily defeat White.

During the 1980s, Clinton accomplished more than just education reform and changes in Arkansas's rural health-care system. He appointed more African Americans to state boards and commissions than all previous Arkansas governors combined. He also appointed the first black lawyer to the state Supreme Court and named an African-American woman to head the state health agency. From 1983, when he was reelected governor, to 1990, when he was completing his fourth term, the unemployment rate in Arkansas dropped from 12 percent to under 7 percent. These and other accomplishments made the ambitious governor of Arkansas an increasingly attractive candidate for the nation's highest office.

The Clintons enjoyed a year of victory in 1992, as Bill achieved his lifelong goal by becoming president of the United States.

7

THE QUEST FOR
THE PRESIDENCY

WITH A FOUR-YEAR TERM of office ahead of him after his election victory in 1986, and no rivals on the political horizon to challenge him in Arkansas, Clinton was able to aim for political goals beyond the state's borders. In the summer of 1986 he was elected chairman of the National Governors Association (NGA). This position allowed him to travel and speak outside of Arkansas and work with governors from across the nation. Clinton used the position to flesh out his theories concerning welfare reform, job creation, and education initiatives while slowly developing new policies and themes. Many of the leading contenders for the 1988 Democratic presidential nomination were members of the association, including Mario Cuomo of New York and Michael Dukakis of Massachusetts.

As President Ronald Reagan neared the end of his second term in office in 1988, he was still very popular with the American electorate. However, the 22nd Amendment to the Constitution prohibits a president from seeking a third term in office. After nearly eight years of Republican rule in the White House, many Democrats were anxious to challenge Vice President George Bush, the Republican candidate for the presidency, in the 1988 general election.

There was speculation about which of the top Democrats would take a shot at the White House. Newspapers in Arkansas, as well as the nationally distributed magazines *Newsweek* and *Time*, had labeled Clinton as a possible contender for his party's presidential nomination. As a seasoned politician, Clinton did nothing to stem these rumors; it was always good to be publicly considered eligible for higher office.

In early 1987, Clinton quietly began to assemble a team that would determine his chances to win the presidency. The presidential candidates for the two major political parties, Republican and Democrat, are selected after a series of primary elections in various states to determine the candidate with the most appeal to members of his party nationally. The primaries culminate in the party's national convention, at which the leading candidate is nominated to run for the presidency and then selects a vice-presidential candidate.

To assess his chances, Clinton covertly sent workers to Iowa and New Hampshire, the two states with the earliest presidential primaries, to poll voters about a possible Clinton candidacy. If Clinton could place first or second in either of these important primary elections, his campaign would receive the national media exposure necessary to win the nomination. A good showing in either of these early contests would also help him raise the millions of dollars in campaign contributions that are necessary to wage a modern-day run for the White House. In April 1987 Clinton visited New Hampshire, and later in the spring he spoke in Iowa and Michigan. He seemed ready to officially announce his candidacy.

A major obstacle was removed from Clinton's path when Arkansas senator Dale Bumpers announced early in the year that he would not seek the presidency in 1988. Bumpers was quite popular with the Arkansas electorate, and Clinton's polls had indicated that the senior senator would triumph against him in a primary. The Democratic State Committee of Arkansas, which had previously backed a Bumpers candidacy, immediately adopted a resolution endorsing Governor Clinton for president. All that was needed now was his official announcement.

Bill Clinton had never shied away from a political challenge and had always dreamed of becoming president of the United States. But he was also a husband and a father, and in 1987 at the age of 41, he decided that his family needed him more than his country.

On July 15, 1987, Governor Clinton called a surprise press conference. He told those gathered that after much soul-searching and many discussions with Hillary he had decided not to seek the Democratic presidential nomination in 1988. Perhaps thinking of his own fatherless childhood, Clinton said:

> My heart says no. . . . I need a little family time. . . . Politicians are people too. I think sometimes we forget it. But they really are. . . . Our daughter is seven. She is the most important person in the world to us and our most important responsibility. In order to wage a winning campaign I would have to go on the road full time from now until the end, and to have Hillary do the same thing. . . . I've seen a lot of kids grow up under these pressures and a long, long time ago I made a promise to myself that if I was ever lucky enough to have a child, she would never grow up wondering who her father was.

With these heartfelt words Clinton took himself out of contention for a goal that he had planned for his entire adult life.

The news that Clinton was not going to seek the presidency surprised most political observers in Arkansas. But the average Arkansan easily identified with a man choosing his family over ambition, and Clinton's decision made him even more popular within his home state. John Brum-

As a leader of Michael Dukakis's 1988 presidential campaign, Bill made many national appearances. After a disastrous speech nominating Dukakis at the Democratic National Convention, Clinton rebounded by impressing Tonight Show *host Johnny Carson with his ability to laugh at himself, as well as with his skill on the saxophone.*

mett of the *Arkansas Gazette*, who often criticized Governor Clinton, told his readers that he believed Clinton was quite sincere in the reasons he gave for not seeking the presidency in 1988.

Bill Clinton had not given up his quest for the presidency, just put it on hold. At age 41, he was still young enough to consider a run in the future. If Vice President George Bush succeeded President Reagan, Clinton could make an attempt in 1992. If a Democrat captured the White House in 1988, Clinton, as a good party man who would not challenge an incumbent Democratic president, would be forced to wait until at least 1996 before he could run for president. In the meantime, he and Hillary would do as they had always done: prepare for the future by working as hard as they could.

Throughout the spring and summer of 1988, Clinton traveled the country campaigning for Massachusetts governor Michael Dukakis, one of the Democratic presidential candidates. He soon became a close advisor to Dukakis, and after the Massachusetts governor had secured the Democratic nomination Dukakis asked Clinton to deliver his nominating speech. Dukakis's decision gave Clinton the opportunity to be viewed by a live national television audience tuned in to the Atlanta convention. In addition, it signaled the delegates that Clinton would play an integral part in the Dukakis administration if the Massachusetts governor attained the presidency.

On July 20, 1988, Governor William Jefferson Clinton stepped up to the podium to deliver the most important speech of his political career. The 35-minute speech, written by Clinton himself, outlined all of Dukakis's qualities. However, as he stepped up to the microphone and looked out on the delegates he knew immediately that something was wrong. The lights, which were usually dimmed when a speech was given, remained brightly shining. As he began to speak, delegates began shouting for Dukakis, and their catcalls and yells threw off Clinton's cadence. Twice he was forced to stop speaking and ask for quiet. Because he was forced to pause so many times, it seemed that the speech went on forever. One newsman, John Chancellor of NBC, told millions of television viewers, "I am afraid Bill Clinton, one of the most attractive governors, just put a blot on his record." The other two networks switched to alternate programs in the middle of his address.

Clinton's seemingly never-ending nominating speech became the butt of jokes throughout the nation. After poking fun at Clinton for almost a week, Johnny Carson, the popular host of the *Tonight Show*, invited the governor to appear on his late-night program. Americans love a politician who can laugh at himself, and Bill Clinton did not disappoint them. Entering the studio with a broad grin on his still-boyish face, Clinton quickly won over his host, telling Carson that the speech was actually a success because it made Dukakis's speech sound that much better, then playing a few tunes on his saxophone with popular band leader Doc Severinsen.

He later told an Arkansas radio host, "If you don't ever fall on your face, you forget how hard life is for a lot of other people all the time." He informed a *Boston Globe* reporter, "It was the worst hour in my life," then immediately added with a self-deprecating laugh, "No, make that an hour and a half."

The 1988 presidential campaign was venomous, with both parties engaging in negative campaigning. On election day George Bush won a decisive victory over Michael Dukakis, capturing 54 percent of the vote to Dukakis's 46 percent and 426 electoral votes to Dukakis's 112.

Although Dukakis's loss was a blow to the Democratic Party, it provided a boost to Bill Clinton's national political hopes; he was immediately labeled a front-runner for the 1992 nomination. Before he could start campaigning, however, he had to decide if he wanted to run for a fifth term as governor of Arkansas in 1990. Presidential campaigns had become full-time affairs lasting up to two years, and Clinton feared that his duties as governor would detract from his presidential effort. In addition, if he was upset by a challenger during the Arkansas gubernatorial election it would cast doubt on his chances for national political success.

Clinton decided to run for a fifth term in spite of these concerns, and he faced Republican challenger Sheffield Nelson, a business executive who ran the state's largest utility, the Arkansas-Louisiana Gas Company. Clinton

Surrounded by his family, Bill Clinton announced his candidacy for president of the United States in the fall of 1991.

won easily, capturing 59 percent of the vote. Having established a secure political base in Arkansas, he could now concentrate on capturing the American presidency.

On October 3, 1991, William Jefferson Clinton stood on the steps of the Arkansas State House with Hillary and Chelsea by his side and announced his intention to seek the Democratic nomination for president. He told the hundreds of friends and supporters who had come to Arkansas from all over the nation:

. . . I stand here today, because I refuse to stand by and let our children become part of the first generation to do worse than their parents. I don't want my child or your child to be part of a country that's coming apart instead of coming together. . . . The country is headed in the wrong direction fast, slipping behind, losing our way, and all we have out of Washington is status quo paralysis. No vision, no action, just neglect, selfishness, and division.

If he were elected president, Clinton said, he would institute a plan he called the New Covenant. This included legislation similar to the GI Bill that would allow any qualified student to borrow money for college and repay it through national service (the original GI Bill had provided money for college and low-interest home mortgages to veterans of World War II); preschool for every child in the nation; apprenticeship programs for those who wanted to learn a trade or craft instead of attending college; middle-class tax relief; elimination of trade barriers; and a pledge to "present a plan to Congress and the American people to provide affordable, quality health care for all Americans."

There were several other Democratic contenders for the party's nomination, including former Massachusetts senator Paul Tsongas; former California governor Jerry Brown; Senator Tom Harkin of Iowa; Nebraska senator Bob Kerrey; and Douglas Wilder, a Virginia state senator. The candidates battled through the state primaries during the spring and early summer, but on the eve of the Democratic National Convention, Clinton had enough support to receive his party's nomination. When he was selected by the delegates at the convention, Clinton chose another southerner, Senator Albert Gore of Tennessee, as his running mate. Gore was a leader in the Senate who was well known as an environmentalist.

As Clinton was being chosen by the Democrats as their presidential nominee, incumbent president George Bush was nominated again by the Republican Party. The Republican National Convention was held in Texas, President

Bill was well liked on the campaign trail, particularly by young people and those hurt by the 1991–92 recession.

Bush's home state, and the delegates unanimously selected him to head the ticket, which he shared again with Vice President Dan Quayle.

Although Bush had the advantage of incumbency, he had some weaknesses. He had been challenged in the Republican primaries, a rare occurrence for a sitting president, by conservative columnist and former presidential speechwriter Patrick Buchanan, who stressed the need for revision of America's trade and immigration policies. Although the president had easily won in the primary because of Buchanan's limited support among voters, the challenge was disturbing.

The American public's general dissatisfaction with politics made the 1992 presidential campaign extremely competitive. Several debates were held in the fall of 1992 between the major candidates: Republican incumbent George Bush, Democrat Bill Clinton, and popular third-party candidate Ross Perot.

Sensing the weak field, as well as a general dissatisfaction with politicians by many Americans, a third candidate entered the race for president. H. Ross Perot, a Texas billionaire, used his vast financial resources to form a new political party, the Patriot Party, and had his name placed on the ballot. Perot campaigned as a practical businessman who was not part of the "beltway crowd," a nickname for people who lived in and around Washington, D.C., which is surrounded by a highway known as the beltway. Perot claimed politicians had lost touch with the average American taxpayer. He proposed an immediate tax increase which would go towards reducing America's growing national debt. Eliminating the debt, he argued, would allow the economy to grow and eventually bring prosperity. Perot's third-party candidacy appealed to the growing number of voters who had become disillusioned with the policies and programs of the two major parties.

During his campaign for reelection, President Bush focused on his foreign policy successes. These included the peaceful end of the "Cold War" between the United States and the Soviet Union, as well as America's role in winning the Gulf War against Iraq in 1991. However, although Bush's handling of the war had resulted in 90 percent approval ratings from the American people, a year later, thanks in large part to a downturn in the U.S. economy, Bush's popularity had plummeted.

Bush also tried to use the tactic that had worked for him in his 1988 presidential campaign: negative campaigning. During the primaries, Clinton's Democratic opponents had raised questions about his avoidance of the draft during the Vietnam War and his alleged drug use and extramarital affairs. Republicans continued the attacks on his character.

- The issue of Clinton's Vietnam draft deferment and his opposition to the war was portrayed as somehow anti-American, as was a visit to Moscow that Clinton had made while a student at Oxford University.

- After years of telling reporters he had never "broken the laws of his country" regarding drugs, Clinton admitted to a reporter that he had tried marijuana once while a student at Oxford, but that he didn't like it and "never inhaled."

- A woman named Gennifer Flowers told the media that she had conducted an affair with Clinton for 12 years. Although Bill and Hillary denied the allegations, other reports indicated that Clinton had conducted numerous affairs while governor of Arkansas. Rumors of infidelity would continue to haunt Clinton for years after the election.

Clinton ignored the attacks on his character, countering by pointing out the effects of 12 years of Republican policy on the American economy. He concentrated on getting out his New Covenant message, and this also helped to highlight the generational differences between Clinton and his opponents, Bush and Perot. Clinton told audiences

Bill Clinton and George Bush walk out of the White House together in January 1993, on their way to Clinton's inauguration as the 42nd president of the United States.

throughout the nation, "The New Covenant means change—change in our party, change in our national leadership, and change in our country."

On the campaign trail, he also observed, "People have lost faith in the ability of government to change their lives for the better. Out there you can hear the quiet, troubled voice of the forgotten middle-class, lamenting that government no longer looks out for their interests or honors their values." As Clinton traveled the country, his message took hold, and he gradually pulled ahead of President Bush in voter polls.

On election day Clinton and Gore defeated their Republican opponents, capturing 43 percent of the popular vote. Bush received 37 percent of the votes and Perot received 19 percent. Clinton and Gore won 378 electoral votes to Bush's 168. Although more than 19 million ballots were cast for Perot, he failed to capture a single electoral vote. At the age of 46 William Jefferson Clinton was the third-youngest man to become president (John F. Kennedy and Theodore Roosevelt were both younger when they attained the presidency).

Clinton had been preparing for the presidency his entire life. His ambitious plans, he hoped, would make life better for all Americans. As he awaited the inauguration, he went about choosing his cabinet and preparing for the transfer of power.

Despite troubles during his first term as president, Bill Clinton retained a warm, open outlook toward the American public.

8

A DIFFICULT
FIRST TERM

THE WEEKS BETWEEN the November presidential election and the inauguration of the chief executive in January are usually taken up with organizing the White House staff, setting the legislative agenda, and choosing the heads of the major federal government departments, collectively known as the president's "cabinet." For the new president, this was a hectic time. President Clinton wanted his cabinet to reflect America's multicultural society, so he chose more women and minorities for top administration posts than any previous president in American history. His appointments included Dr. Jocelyn Elders as surgeon general; Michael Espy, an African-American congressman, as secretary of agriculture; Hispanic Americans Henry Cisneros as secretary of housing and urban development and Fedrico Pena as secretary of transportation; Janet Reno as attorney general; and Ron Brown as secretary of commerce.

Although he had been involved with politics for most of his life, Clinton was inexperienced at dealing with the intricacies of Washington's established bureaucracies. He was always more comfortable

Bill Clinton congratulates Ron Brown, who became secretary of the Commerce Department during Clinton's first term. With them are Vice President Al Gore and Thomas "Mack" McLarty, a close friend of Clinton who was named his administration's chief of staff. Brown was killed in a plane crash in 1996 while working towards negotiating peace in Bosnia.

around the people he had grown up with in Arkansas or gone to school with at Georgetown, Oxford, and Yale, and as president-elect he asked many of these friends to come to Washington and help him serve their country.

Clinton chose Thomas "Mack" McLarty, a childhood friend who was serving as the top executive of Arkansas's largest natural gas company, as his chief of staff. Economist Robert Reich, another close friend who attended Oxford with Clinton in the 1960s and advised him during his campaign for the presidency, was offered the position of secretary of labor. He gladly accepted the president's call to public service.

Clinton organized his White House staff much as former presidents Franklin D. Roosevelt and Lyndon Johnson had.

He blurred the lines of organization among his staffers, with the result that all major decisions had to made by him. In cabinet meetings and informal gatherings in the Oval Office (the president's official office), Clinton allowed his advisors to argue among themselves while he listened, so that he could consider every possible viewpoint.

On January 20, 1993, William Jefferson Clinton, with Hillary at his side holding the family Bible, was sworn in as the nation's 42nd chief executive. Bill Clinton had reached the pinnacle of American electoral politics, and he intended to create a legacy of legislative achievement that would leave its mark on generations to come. Unlike President Bush, who had concentrated most of his energies on foreign policy initiatives, President Clinton had promised the American people that during his first administration he would "put America's house in order" by concentrating almost solely on domestic policy concerns.

During the next two years the Clinton administration would deluge Congress with a legislative agenda that included economic reform, a new student loan program, a family leave policy, reform of the banking and health-care systems, the North American Free Trade Agreement, and a national service program.

In his inaugural speech, President Clinton told the nation that among the most important items on his political agenda were reducing a deficit in the federal budget and improving America's economy. During the final year of George Bush's term as president, the nation had experienced its slowest period of economic growth since the 1930s, and the federal deficit had increased to over $60 billion a year. By the end of the century, the deficit was expected to be over $500 billion. In his speech, Clinton prescribed "sacrifice"—meaning new taxes—to reduce the deficit and jump-start the economy, but he did not give specifics.

On February 17, 1993, Clinton revealed his economic plan before Congress. He proposed spending cuts in the

Bill Clinton often met challenges and was forced to compromise when dealing with the American military. During a visit to warring Bosnia, Clinton praised American soldiers stationed there in the peace effort. However, he was blamed when 18 American soldiers were killed during a peacekeeping mission in Somalia, and his effort to open the military to homosexuals drew criticism.

budget, increased taxes for wealthy Americans, and a $31 billion "economic stimulus package" that included funds for public works, education, health care, and welfare reform.

Although Clinton's plan to reduce the budget deficit struck a chord with the American people, his economic stimulus package was opposed by many congressional leaders. Because of political opposition, the stimulus package was scaled back to $16.3 billion in incentives. Although the bill passed in the House of Representatives, it failed to pass in the Senate. Four months later, a scaled-down bill, including a 4.3-cent increase in the gas tax and a strategy to reduce the deficit by $500 billion over five years, passed by one vote.

Another of Clinton's early battles concerned allowing homosexuals to serve in America's armed forces. In the past, any man or woman serving in the military who admitted to being homosexual was discharged. The gay community had supported Clinton and the Democratic Party in the 1992 elections because Clinton viewed this practice as a violation of civil rights laws and proposed opening the military to all qualified citizens, regardless of their sexual orientation.

Clinton's proposal was met by stiff opposition both from the military and from congressional leaders of both parties. Georgia senator Sam Nunn, the powerful Democratic chairman of the Armed Services Committee, openly opposed the president, and General Colin Powell, the highly respected chairman of the Joint Chiefs of Staff, the top U.S. military leaders, also resisted the new plan.

Because Clinton hoped to pass so much new legislation, including health care and education reform, he decided to walk away from this battle. Instead, the military initiated a "don't ask, don't tell" policy, meaning that soldiers would not be asked about their sexual orientation but could still be mustered out of the military if they were openly homosexual. Although this was far from the solution that the president had wanted, in a speech before a predominantly military audience Clinton said that the policy "is not a perfect solution. . . . [but] it is an honorable compromise." It was not the last time he would have to compromise his high-minded ideals as president.

The change in position on the issue, which occurred in the first few weeks of Clinton's term, hurt him politically; one poll showed a 20 percent drop in his favorability ratings.

Clinton was more successful in passing two pieces of new legislation early in 1993: the Family and Medical Leave Act, which required companies to give their workers up to 12 weeks per year of unpaid medical leave to care for a newborn or newly adopted child or to take care of a sick family member; and the National Voter Registration

One of Clinton's greatest foreign policy victories may have been the peace treaty signed in 1995 by Israel and the Palestine Liberation Organization (PLO), which led to cessation of hostilities in the troubled Middle East.

Act, known as the "motor-voter bill," which allowed people to register to vote when they applied for a driver's license. Both of these bills had been vetoed by President Bush in the past; this time, they passed in Congress with wide margins and Clinton signed them into law.

Clinton was also able to develop a new program in 1993. AmeriCorps was called "a domestic Peace Corps" by the president, and modeled after the program started by President Kennedy in the 1960s. In the Peace Corps, young Americans earned money and experience by teaching in undeveloped "Third World" countries. Clinton's program allowed students to earn money for college, or to repay student loans, through service in America's inner cities and rural communities. Although it was criticized by Republicans, the program brought thousands of young, enthusiastic workers into areas that sorely needed their help.

Although Bill Clinton had promised to focus his attention on domestic policy, international events forced him to make important foreign policy decisions early in his term.

During the presidential transition, President Bush, in cooperation with the United Nations, sent a small contingent of American combat troops to the African nation of Somalia on a humanitarian mission. The people of Somalia were facing a famine, and warring factions were preventing food and medicine from reaching the country's starving populace. Clinton supported President Bush's decision to use American troops for the mission.

When Clinton entered the White House, United States troops were still stationed in Somalia carrying out humanitarian duties, even though as the famine subsided many members of Congress demanded the immediate withdrawal of all American troops. Tragedy occurred in October 1993, when 18 U.S. soldiers were killed while trying to capture a leader of one of the warring clans. Under intense pressure from members of both parties, Clinton was forced to withdraw all American troops from Somalia. Secretary of Defense Les Aspin resigned his post shortly thereafter. Although he had inherited the Somalia situation from his predecessor, the episode left a blemish on Clinton's foreign policy record.

His initiatives in the divided nation once known as Yugoslavia would be solely of his own making. In 1991 ethnic violence erupted in Bosnia, where the Serbian population was undertaking a program of "ethnic cleansing," a euphemism for mass murder, of the country's Muslim minority. The United States had condemned the atrocities but refrained from using the military to intervene. After almost 20 years America was still divided by its involvement in Vietnam, and U.S. military leaders were opposed to a military conflict as complex as the situation in Bosnia.

President Clinton and Secretary of State Warren Christopher brokered a Bosnian cease-fire in 1995 and subsequently sent 20,000 American combat troops to Bosnia as part of a North Atlantic Treaty Organization (NATO) peacekeeping operation to stop the ethnic cleansing. Although the presence of troops did prevent some bloodshed, the Serbs continued to attack Muslim cities that had been designated "safe areas" in the treaty.

Another issue that had both national and global ramifications was the passage in 1994 of the North American Free Trade Agreement (NAFTA). The agreement was intended to improve trade between the United States, Canada, and Mexico. However, there was opposition to the trade agreement, particularly from labor unions, a major supporter of Clinton and the Democratic Party. The union leaders believed that if NAFTA passed, American companies would move manufacturing jobs to Mexico, where they could produce goods more cheaply than in the United States. This would cost the United States jobs. Ross Perot led the opposition to NAFTA, claiming that the deal would destroy the American middle class. Clinton worked with Republicans in Congress, who supported the trade agreement, and it passed easily.

The year had not started so well, however; on January 6, 1994, less than a year into his presidency, Bill's mother Virginia passed away in her sleep. The president was devastated by her death. Hillary had lost her father to cancer during the first year of the administration, and together the Clintons attempted to ease their grief by concentrating on their work.

During Bill Clinton's first term as president, his main legislative task was a mammoth one: creation of a plan that would provide affordable health care for all Americans. As he had in Arkansas, President Clinton put the legislative project that was most important to him into the hands of his wife, Hillary, who chaired a task force charged with designing a national health-care plan.

National health insurance had a long political history in the United States. In 1912 Theodore Roosevelt ran on a Progressive Party platform that included national health care as one of its planks. President Harry S. Truman had introduced his version of national health care during his second term in office, but it was quickly labeled "socialized medicine" by the powerful American Medical Association. Presidents Johnson and Nixon had also proposed forms of national health insurance, but both presidents were quickly forced to back away from the subject when insurance and pharmaceutical lobbyists rallied in opposition.

Reforming the health-care industry would take a major effort. In 1993, 37 million Americans had no health insurance and another 35 million had less than adequate coverage. Providing coverage to them and simultaneously broadening other forms of care was estimated to cost a minimum of $50 billion a year. And the cost of providing health care

The most important initiative during the first term of Bill Clinton's presidency was an effort to reform the nation's health-care system. He appointed his wife, Hillary Rodham Clinton, to chair a committee charged with creating a reform plan in 1993. Hillary is shown here meeting with the health subcommittee of the Congressional Black Caucus.

was rising annually by an estimated $100 billion.

In the months after the inauguration, Mrs. Clinton traveled all over the country attending meetings, gathering information, and lobbying for change. Polls showed that many Americans favored reform.

On September 22, 1993, the health-care task force presented the Health Security Act to Congress. The bill, they said, would slow the rapidly rising cost of health care and provide universal insurance coverage.

The Clinton plan immediately faced stiff opposition from a number of organizations. The American Medical Association, which represented a majority of American doctors, viewed any national program of health insurance as a threat to its members. Conservative Republicans in Congress opposed any new federal programs that would increase the budget deficit. The health-insurance industry feared a loss of revenue if it had to compete against an inexpensive federal program. Even some members of Clinton's own party opposed the plan, fearing that a sustained battle over health-care reform would hurt the party politically in the 1994 Congressional election.

Although Republicans in Congress might have agreed to some of the provisions in the bill, President Clinton promised that he would veto any scaled-down bill that did not include universal health coverage. After a year of debate over the Health Security Act, during which Congress did not vote on the legislation, the administration decided to give up the fight for universal health care.

The Clinton administration's failure to pass the major items on its ambitious legislative agenda, such as health-care reform and the economic stimulus package, were compounded by several scandals, ranging from the trivial (air traffic at a Los Angeles airport was delayed while Clinton received a $200 haircut from a trendy stylist) to the serious (the firing of seven employees in the White House travel office). Several of Clinton's nominees for high government positions withdrew their names from consideration under intense media scrutiny. But the most important scandal that broke in 1993 was Whitewater.

In 1978, the Clintons had become partners with Jim and Susan McDougal to develop land near the White River in Arkansas. Bill Clinton was governor of Arkansas at the time, and Hillary Rodham was working at the Rose Law Firm. For years, the Clintons had maintained that they had lost nearly $70,000 in the deal. Republican opponents of the Clinton administration charged that Bill and Hillary had acted illegally, using their positions to help their partner, Jim McDougal, who had dealt with the Whitewater Development Corporation through his savings and loan, Madison Guaranty. Madison failed in 1989; this cost taxpayers $60 million and led to criminal charges against McDougal, of which he was acquitted. Hillary Rodham Clinton had represented McDougal's savings and loan on occasion and at one point intervened with a Clinton-appointed regulator on a questionable stock scheme that McDougal had proposed.

Six months after the Clintons moved into the White House, a close friend and former Rose Law Firm partner, Vincent Foster, was found dead in a Virginia park, an apparent suicide. Foster, a White House deputy counsel, had kept a file detailing the Clintons' involvement in Whitewater, but the file was missing from his office after his death. It was later turned over to Justice Department investigators, but the public perception was that the Clintons were covering something up.

The scandal caused the media to ask if the Clintons had committed any crimes in their Whitewater dealings or if it was simply a bad investment. The Justice Department even authorized an independent counsel to investigate the allegations of wrongdoing. By the spring of 1994, this failed real estate deal threatened to immobilize the Clinton White House, and the administration's problems led to reduced confidence in the young president.

As a result, the Republican Party, under the leadership

Bill Clinton is shown shaking hands with Newt Gingrich, the Republican Speaker of the House, in 1995. After overwhelming Republican success in 1994 congressional election, President Clinton made tentative steps towards forging bipartisan ties.

of Georgia representative Newt Gingrich, swept both houses of Congress in the 1994 elections. Not since the Republican administration of Dwight D. Eisenhower in 1952 had the Republicans captured both houses of Congress simultaneously. Republicans outnumbered Democrats 52-48 in the Senate and 230-204 in the House.

To many observers, the off-year election was a repudiation of Clinton and his policies. The president had run in 1992 as a "New Democrat," but by 1994 the Republicans had been able to portray President Clinton as another "tax and spend Democrat"; consequently they had won a historic political victory.

After the 1994 election, when Clinton was asked by historian James McGregor Burns how he planned to pass his legislative agenda through a hostile Congress, the president's pat answer reflected both his political and his personal philosophy: "Just keep going at them until they tire." But the truth was that President Clinton's political power was at its lowest point, and he would have to adjust his goals for America's future in order to deal with the new reality of a Republican Congress.

The Clinton family waves to the crowd during the 1996 presidential campaign. Clinton won a second term, running on the concept that his presidency would build "a bridge to the 21st century."

9

SECOND-TERM COMEBACK

FOR THE SECOND two years of his term, President Clinton's job would be more difficult because he would be dealing with a Republican-dominated Congress that was opposed to many of his programs and plans. The new Speaker of the House, Newt Gingrich, and other Republicans had run on a platform dubbed the "Contract with America" that promised a balanced budget amendment to the Constitution, welfare reform, giving the president the power to veto items in the budget to reduce wasteful spending, and reduced taxes for families.

Within the first 100 days of the 104th session of Congress, the Republicans in the House, led by the 73 freshman congressman who had been elected in November 1994, had brought the 10 major bills outlined in the Contract with America up for a vote and passed most of them.

Clinton's popularity had reached the lowest point of his presidency, and there was some talk among Democrats about challenging him for the presidency in 1996. A sitting president is rarely challenged in his party's primary, so the news that powerful Democratic congressman Richard Gephardt was considering running for the White House

97

On a hot August day, Clinton meets his supporters during the 1996 campaign.

was reflective of how Clinton's political stock had fallen.

However, the Republican-majority Congress proved to be a blessing in disguise for Clinton. The Senate, traditionally more conservative than the House, declined to vote on several of the proposals outlined in the Contract with America, and those that Congress did pass were vetoed by the president. This gave Clinton supporters an opportunity to challenge the common perception that the president did not have principals and would not take a politically unpopular stand. In addition, the unwillingness of the Republican Party (or GOP, for Grand Old Party) to compromise was a tactical error that would allow Clinton to regain popularity in the final two years of his term.

When Republicans refused in late 1995 to approve the Clinton administration's 1996 budget, the federal government was forced to shut down in November 1995. Over 280,000 workers were temporarily laid off because the government could not pay them, and another 500,000 federal employees were required to work without pay because their department budgets had not been approved. The shutdown affected the lives of many Americans by stopping services such as Meals on Wheels, closing federal parks and monuments, slowing processing of small business loans and government mortgage insurance, and interfering with federal hazardous waste cleanups and water safety monitoring.

Two months later, the Republicans forced another government shutdown, this one for several weeks. Again, federal services were stopped or slowed by the shutdown. As a result, Republicans were portrayed in the media as taking a hard line that was detrimental to the country's best interests, while Clinton was praised as willing to compromise.

The GOP's image was also damaged by its proposal to cut spending for Medicare, a federal program that provides basic health insurance for senior citizens, and Medicaid, a similar program that assists low-income citizens. When Clinton vetoed Republican legislation that would have reduced spending on these programs, known as entitlements, his stock rose among older voters. Clinton was also praised for vetoing several other GOP-sponsored bills.

"The knock on Bill Clinton was that he didn't stand for anything, wouldn't fight for anything," a Democratic pollster, Mark Mellman, said later in an assessment of the second half of Clinton's first term. "The Republicans handed him the opportunity to be seen as resolute, firm, fighting on behalf of average working people. That changed the political landscape and the political dynamic in his favor."

At the same time that Clinton was reinventing himself politically, Gingrich went from being one of the most popular political leaders in the nation to one of the most unpopular. Complaints that he used his power as Speaker of the House improperly led to the appointment of a House panel to investigate Gingrich's ethics. Ultimately, the panel found that he may have violated campaign finance laws by using money from GOPAC, the polical action committee that he oversaw, to fund a college course that he taught, and Gingrich was assessed a $300,000 penalty. When compared to Gingrich, President Clinton appeared to be a moderate conciliator.

One of President Clinton's brightest foreign policy achievements occurred during the second half of his first term, when he helped to broker an agreement between Israel and Palestinians that would end Israel's nearly 30-year military occupation of the West Bank and provide a foundation for the creation of a Palestinian state. Israeli prime minister Yitzhak Rabin and Palestine Liberation Organization (PLO) chairman Yasser Arafat signed the historic agreement in Washington, D.C., on September 28, 1995, and urged other Middle Eastern nations, such as Syria and Lebanon, to take part in the peace process as well. Both also condemned terrorism in the region. "Chapter by chapter, Jews and Arabs are writing a new history for their ancient lands," Clinton said at the signing ceremony.

As a result, as 1996 began Clinton's popularity had increased and there was no more talk of a Democratic primary challenge. With the American economy in good shape, another positive for the incumbent president, Clinton was free to pursue his legislative agenda and focus his reelection efforts against his Republican rival, who would be selected during the punishing spring primary season.

At the Republican convention in San Diego in August 1996, Senate majority leader Robert Dole was selected as the GOP's presidential candidate. Dole had survived strong challenges from conservative Pat Buchanan and millionare publisher Steve Forbes during the primary. He selected Jack Kemp, a former congressman and Reagan cabinet member, as his running mate.

Dole, who relinquished his Senate seat to devote himself full-time to the campaign, had been former president Gerald Ford's running mate in 1976 and an unsuccessful presidential candidate in 1980 and 1988. Dole was a veteran of World War II and had been severely wounded in battle, forever losing the use of his right arm.

Although Dole was well qualified for the office of the presidency, at age 73 he was considered by many to be too old to lead the nation into the next century. Dole was a member of John F. Kennedy's and George Bush's generation, and with Bush's loss in 1992, the reins of government, it seemed, had already been passed to the younger generation represented by Clinton.

Dole also was at a disadvantage because he had spent most of his campaign funds to win the Republican nomination. He did not have enough money to counter Clinton political advertisements on television. The Democratic National Party also ran "issue ads" targeted to help Democratic candidates in key areas, and these advertisements hurt Dole's campaign.

Ross Perot again entered the race as an independent candidate, and although he did not do as well in his second campaign as he had in his first, he still pulled many votes that otherwise probably would have gone to Dole.

In the end, Clinton won the 1996 election fairly easily, with 276 electoral votes to Dole's 156. He received 49 percent of the popular vote, with Dole garnering 41 percent and Perot 8 percent. However, the President failed to translate his popularity into votes for Democratic members of Congress; the Republicans maintained their control of the House and Senate.

In his second term, President Clinton made racial harmony and national service two of his major goals.

Racial harmony has been a topic of discussion since before the civil rights movement of the 1960s. Clinton, who grew up personally viewing the negative consequences of racism in the South, decided that in his second term he would attempt to address the divisions between the races in the United States.

In a June 1997 speech, Clinton announced a national initiative on race relations, calling for a year-long focus on racial issues. He also appointed a seven-member commission to study race relations and moderated a nationally televised discussion on race, held in Akron, Ohio, in December 1997. The Akron town meeting was intended as the first of many meetings and discussions to be held across the country in 1998.

"It is really potentially a great thing for America that we are becoming so multiethnic at the time the world is becoming so closely tied together," Clinton told the American Society of Newspaper Editors in 1997. "But it's also potentially a powder keg of problems and heartbreak and division and loss."

The president had referred to a "season of service" for all Americans during his first inaugural address. During his second term, in an effort to promote national service and improve the quality of life for millions of Americans, the president appointed Colin Powell, the former chairman of the Joint Chiefs of Staff, to chair a committee on increasing volunteerism. Powell hosted a summit in Philadelphia during the spring of 1997 to promote volunteer work.

Domestically, Clinton was praised as the fiscal restraint of his administration began to bear fruit. In January 1998 the administration proposed the first "balanced" budget in over 25 years. That is, the U.S. could cover all of its spending for the year with the revenue it would bring in from taxes, and would not add to the national debt.

Clinton's foreign policy decisions during his second term, particularly in the Middle East, were supported by the American public. In the fall of 1997, Iraq's president, Saddam Hussein, refused to allow United Nations inspectors to enter several sites where the U.N. believed chemical weapons were being developed. This was a violation of a cease-fire signed after Iraq was defeated by U.N.-led forces during the Gulf War. Hussein had remained in power despite tight economic sanctions that made life miserable for the average citizen of Iraq.

The U.N. condemned Hussein's actions, and Clinton ordered American troops and warships into the Persian Gulf in case the situation escalated. However, Russian negotiators brokered a new agreement and the U.N. inspectors were allowed to continue their work.

President Clinton also attempted to preserve the Middle East peace accord signed between Israel and Palestinians two years earlier. The agreement signed by Israeli prime minister Yitzhak Rabin and Palestinian leader Yasser Arafat in September 1995 had nearly collapsed following the assassination of Rabin in November and the ascension to power of Benjamin Netanyahu, a hard-line Israeli

Bill Clinton is sworn in for a second term as president by Supreme Court Chief Justice William Rehnquist in January 1997. He named equal opportunity, volunteerism, and racial understanding as goals for his second term.

Bill Clinton, shown here with Chelsea in 1993, has always recognized the strength of family. In the fall of 1997, Bill and Hillary felt the separation keenly as they watched their daughter begin college at Stanford University.

nationalist. As 1998 began the president attempted to set up a meeting between Netanyahu and Arafat so that the peace process could proceed.

With these commendable domestic and foreign policy initiatives and a continued strong economy, Bill Clinton's job approval rating, which reflects positive public opinion of his decisions and policies, was over 65 percent at the end of 1997—at one of the highest points in his presidency. However, events in his personal life would soon change the public's perception of the president.

Early in Clinton's first term, the *American Spectator* published remarks by an Arkansas state trooper that Clinton had had several sexual affairs while he was governor and that the trooper had brought women to him in hotels, including a woman named "Paula" in 1991. After the story broke, Paula Jones, a former Arkansas state employee, said that she had been taken to a hotel room to meet the governor but denied that she had engaged in consensual sex with Clinton. Jones claimed that the governor had made improper sexual advances, which she had rebuffed, and she sued both the newly elected president and the state trooper who had made the initial allegation, citing defamation of character.

President Clinton's lawyers argued that the civil lawsuit should not be heard until after the president was out of office, but the U.S. Supreme Court ruled that the lawsuit should proceed, and a trial was set for May 1998. Clinton was required to give information in response to Jones's lawyers' questions, known as a deposition, at the beginning of January 1998.

Two weeks after his deposition, Clinton came under intense media scrutiny when a former Pentagon aide, Linda Tripp, gave Kenneth Starr, the independent counsel investigating the Clintons' involvement in Whitewater and other scandals, audiotapes of a conversation with a former White House intern who claimed she had had a sexual affair with the president three years earlier. Starr, who had been inves-

tigating the Clintons' involvement in Whitewater for nearly four years, received approval from Attorney General
Janet Reno to broaden his probe into the new allegations.
At issue was whether the president and a close advisor, Ver-
non Jordan, had told the former intern, Monica Lewinsky,
to lie about the affair in order to protect Clinton during the
Jones lawsuit. Lewinsky had denied the rumor while under
oath during her deposition in the Jones case, and Clinton
had claimed that he had not had affairs with women while
in the White House. The charges of lying under oath, or
perjury, and conspiring to obstruct justice by telling Lewinsky to lie, were serious enough that talk began to circulate
about possible impeachment proceedings if the story could
be proved. However, the president, his wife, and his staff
stood by his statement that he had not had an affair and had
done nothing improper.

On April 1, 1998, the federal judge presiding over the
Paula Jones civil case threw out the lawsuit, saying that
Jones's lawyers had "failed to demonstrate that she has a
case" for discrimination or sexual harassment. Clinton's
supporters felt the dismissal vindicated the president;
however, independent counsel Kenneth Starr said that he
would continue his investigations into the allegation that
the president tampered with Lewinsky's testimony and was
involved in Whitewater and other scandals.

When President Clinton leaves office in the year 2001,
he will be only 55 years old. He could be tapped for a seat
on the United States Supreme Court, or serve the country
as a roving ambassador of peace, as former president
Jimmy Carter has done since leaving office. Or, he could
choose to remain in American government by seeking a
seat in the U.S. Senate or House of Representatives, as
another former president, John Quincy Adams, did over
150 years ago. However, whatever road Bill Clinton
chooses to take, there is no doubt that he will continue to
make an important contribution to the country he has
served with such dedication for his entire adult life.

CHRONOLOGY

1946   William Jefferson (Bill) Blythe II killed in a car accident May 17; William Jefferson Blythe III (later known as Bill Clinton) born August 19

1963   While attending Boys' Nation in Washington, D.C., meets President John F. Kennedy

1964   Graduates from Hot Springs High School; enters Georgetown University

1966   Attains a part-time position on the staff of the Senate Foreign Relations Committee

1968   Graduates from Georgetown; wins a Rhodes Scholarship to Oxford University

1971   Enters law school at Yale University

1973   Earns law degree from Yale

1975   Marries Hillary Rodham October 11

1974   Loses first election, for Arkansas Third District seat in the U.S. House of Representatives

1976   Elected attorney general of Arkansas; runs Georgia governor Jimmy Carter's presidential campaign in Arkansas

1978   Elected governor of Arkansas, becoming the youngest governor in the United States; becomes partner in Whitewater Development Corporation

1980   Daughter Chelsea Victoria Clinton is born February 27; loses reelection bid to Frank White

1982   Reelected governor, defeating Frank White

1984   Reelected governor, defeating Woody Freeman

1986   Reelected governor, this time for a four-year term

1990   Reelected governor; says he will serve entire four-year term in Arkansas

1991   Announces candidacy for president of the United States on October 3

1992   Elected president of the United States, defeating incumbent George Bush

1993   Appoints Hillary Rodham Clinton to chair task force exploring health-care reform; passes Medical Leave Act and "motor-voter" legislation

1994   Hits low point in presidency as Republicans win both houses of Congress for the first time in 40 years

1996   Reelected president, becoming the first Democrat since Franklin Delano Roosevelt to be elected to a full second term

1997   Praised for initiatives on race and national service; U.S. Supreme Court sets May 1998 date for Paula Jones lawsuit

1998   Under fire for Monica Lewinsky scandal; pressures Iraq to comply with U.N. inspections of suspected chemical weapons manufacturing facilities

FURTHER READING

Allen, Charles F., and Jonathan Portis. *The Comeback Kid: The Life and Career of Bill Clinton*. New York: Birch Lane Press, 1992.

Cambell, Colin, & Bert A. Rockman, eds. *The Clinton Presidency: First Appraisals*. Chatham, N.J.: Chatham House Publishers, 1996.

Drew, Elizabeth. *On the Edge: The Clinton Presidency*. New York: Simon & Schuster, 1994.

Kelley, Virginia with James Morgan. *Leading with My Heart*. New York: Simon & Schuster, 1994.

Maraniss, David. *First in His Class: A Biography of Bill Clinton*. New York: Simon & Schuster, 1995.

Morris, Roger. *Partners in Power: The Clintons and Their America*. New York: Henry Holt, 1996.

Renshon, Stanley A. *High Hopes: The Clinton Presidency and the Politics of Ambition*. New York: New York University Press, 1996.

Woodward, Bob. *The Agenda: Inside the Clinton White House*. New York: Simon & Schuster, 1994.

INDEX

PICTURE CREDITS

MICHAEL KELLY is a historian who has taught at the City College of New York and the State University of New York at Stony Brook. A former recipient of the Excellence Award at CCNY, which is awarded to the top graduate student, Michael has received research grants from the Truman Presidential Library and the Eisenhower Presidential Library. He is the author of numerous articles on American politics, including "The 1920 Presidential Election," and has written several books, including a biography of U.S. Senator Jacob K. Javits.

JAMES SCOTT BRADY serves on the board of trustees with the Center to Prevent Handgun Violence and is the Vice Chairman of the Brain Injury Foundation. Mr. Brady served as Assistant to the President and White House Press Secretary under President Ronald Reagan. He was severely injured in an assassination attempt on the president, but remained the White House Press Secretary until the end of the administration. Since leaving the White House, Mr. Brady has lobbied for stronger gun laws. In November 1993, President Bill Clinton signed the Brady Bill, a national law requiring a waiting period on handgun purchases and a background check on buyers.